Praise for *Searching for Grasshopper*

"Cathy Chapaty's *Searching for Grasshopper* is a powerfully transparent book about one's challenging journey through life and how martial arts influence helped her become the person she is today."

—**Melody Shuman**
Founder,
SkillzWorldwide

"It's one part memoir, one part training manual, especially for anyone taking an emotional journey through the martial arts. Cathy has had an amazing life. She survived abuse, alcoholism, homophobia, spiritual turmoil, and depression. Mentors failed her, but she didn't give up. Black eyes and bruises didn't hold her back. She faced her fears in the ring and on the street."

—**Alex Gillis**
Author of *A Killing Art:
The Untold History of Tae Kwon Do*

"Martial arts are known for enriching one's life through self-discovery. It's not all about the fight but more so a metaphor of one conquering one's struggles in life. That is the true battle. In this beautifully written memoir, Cathy Chapaty has laid everything bare. From her life growing up and how it shaped her to be an introverted young woman to all the trials and tribulations that martial arts training helped her conquer, she has covered it all. Martial arts are about self-defense from aggression, self-defense from external attack. Cathy Chapaty shows us the real value in learning martial arts—self-defense from and conquering internal attack. For all of us, this is where the real battle lies. The battle is not won in one major engagement but in the series of victories accumulated. Cathy tells us of hers in vivid detail. The wins, losses, the struggles. This book is an inspiration for us all."

—**Dan Anderson**
Seventh-degree black belt in karate,
four-time national karate champion,
and author of more than forty books on martial arts

Praise for *Searching for Grasshopper*

"*Searching for Grasshopper* is a straight-from-the-heart account of a martial artist's journey—not a quest so much as a question: What is next for me? Chapaty layers her life's discoveries and accomplishments among her old habits and fears, seeking meaning from the contrasts. Her story illustrates a valuable lesson for martial artists and others: That our past is always with us, yet we can only move forward."

—Susan Schorn
Author of *Smile at Strangers:*
And Other Lessons in the Art of Living Fearlessly

"Like life, learning the martial arts has many paths, many journeys, many pitfalls, and many rewards. This book brings to life the journey of one individual who was able to accomplish a passion which was inspired by the 1970s TV series *Kung Fu*. As Kwai Chang Caine, affectionately referred to as Grasshopper, set out for his journey, Cathy set out for hers. You will enjoy reading this book!"

—Michael Matsuda
President, Martial Arts History Museum

SEARCHING
FOR
GRASSHOPPER

A MARTIAL ARTIST'S QUEST FOR PEACE

CATHY CHAPATY

Dudley Dog Press
Austin, Texas

Dudley Dog Press
P.O. Box 16516
Austin, Texas 78761

Published in 2019
Printed and distributed in the United States of America
ISBN 13: 978-1723095603
ISBN 10: 1723095605

Cover photo and design by Callie Jo Prather
Author photo by Kim Johnson

Some names and identifying characteristics have been changed to protect identities.

*Dedicated to martial artists around the world
who bow onto mats every day, seeking to improve themselves, face and
defeat their dragons, and make the world a better, more just place.*

A deep bow to you all.

Contents

Foreword

ONE of my greatest memories and happiest moments was when I was involved with filming the ABC Movie of the Week *Kung Fu*. This great television show and series inspired many people and helped them understand the beautiful concept of the Shaolin Temple's teaching: uniting the mind, body, and spirit.

The series helped people worldwide to understand inner peace of the body and mind by using common sense and logic:

- Be nonviolent until it is necessary to use force.
- Use the mind to understand the way of life toward all living beings and creatures.
- Develop the body to withstand all hardship, whether physical or mental.

MORE than forty years later, I still get letters, messages, and emails regarding this great show, which led people to begin studying the various martial arts systems that were offered in their area. (Back then, Kung Fu schools were limited, so many other martial arts reaped the wealth and knowledge of this far-reaching show.)

I hope that this book will help inspire you to seek and practice a martial art. No matter what system it may be, knowledge is neutral. It is up to each person to utilize the benefits for yourself and your loved ones.

Sifu Douglas Wong

Part I

The Search Begins

The Grasshopper Seed

CAINE, a Shaolin Temple priest who fled to the West, had just killed a bounty hunter in the final scene of a TV movie called *Kung Fu*.

It was the winter of 1972. I sat on the cold hardwood floor of my family's living room, my butt sore and my numb legs shooting painful daggers down to my heels. But I never took my eyes off the screen. I was in awe of what I was watching on the rabbit-eared antennae-topped television.

"What will you do?" a railroad worker asked Caine in the final scene.

Caine's reply was calm, serene, and simple:

"Work. Wander. Rest when I can."

THE premiere of *Kung Fu* had ended. Mamma turned off the television. Yet I continued to stare as the little white beam in the center of the television screen faded until all I could see was my dark reflection. This particular television was the wicked object that Mamma despised—Daddy's bygones gift for his latest drunk driving arrest. But that night it was a portal that opened a new world.

Kung Fu told the story of Kwai Chang Caine, a half-American, half-Chinese orphan boy who became a Buddhist priest and an expert martial artist in the Shaolin Temple. Every image of the film—from the opening scene of Caine walking through the desert at sunset amid beautiful guzheng strumming to his teachers' wise words—was salve for my already-tired, nine-year-old soul.

Watching the movie, I was no longer in San Antonio. I no longer

1

smelled the stench of Daddy's last swig of whiskey. I was transported to China. As if in the movie myself, I stood in the rain outside the monastery gates for days with young Caine, waiting for the abbot to invite him into the temple. When Master Teh finally asked young Caine and others to come inside, I followed and was immediately mesmerized by the candlelit temple. It felt so much safer than the harsh outside world.

I stood beside Master Teh as he gave young Caine his first lesson:

"Quick as you can: Snatch the pebble from my hand," Master Teh said.

Young Caine was too slow.

"When you can take the pebble from my hand, it will be time for you to leave."

I wanted a nickname like "Grasshopper," given young Caine by the old, wise, white-bearded, and white-eyed Master Po. When Po asked Caine to close his eyes and listen to the world, Caine heard only the birds and water.

"Do you hear the grasshopper, which is at your feet?" Master Po asked.

A surprised Caine opened his eyes to see a grasshopper by his toes.

"Old man, how is it that you hear these things?" Caine asked.

"Young man, how is it that you do not?" Master Po replied.

I was hooked. I soaked up every one of Grasshopper's lessons. The spiritual truths resonated; I was so hungry for peace and serenity. And I was sad when the now-older student Caine finally snatched the pebble from Master Teh's hand. I wanted Grasshopper to remain at the temple. *I* wanted to remain at the temple—that is until the next scene. Caine approached a large, black cauldron filled with hot coals. The cauldron bore raised imprints of a dragon on one side and a tiger on the other. To leave the temple, students had to move the cauldron using only their forearms, burning the sign of the Shaolin priesthood into their flesh. Caine easily moved the cauldron.

"Whoa…" I gasped.

I immediately wanted *that*, not really knowing or understanding yet what *that* was.

"TIME for bed," Mamma said, jolting me back to reality in the family living room.

I rose from the floor and dragged my numb foot to my bedroom. For months afterward, I sat down religiously to watch every episode of *Kung Fu*. Instantly fascinated by Asian culture, customs, and rituals, I yearned to go through a similar rite of passage like Grasshopper did at the Shaolin monastery. That sixty minutes a week was my chance to live vicariously through Caine, dreaming of the day I'd be tall, strong, and courageous enough to trudge a journey of my own. I longed to be brave, to defend the meek of the world, to defend myself. I wanted to shave my head and live at that distant, mysterious, and magical Shaolin Temple. I wanted to live anywhere other than our drama-filled home. I wanted to be graceful, peaceful, and wise. I wanted to be anyone but myself. And, boy, did I wish I could beat the snot out of my teasing, bullying classmates at school like Caine did the bad guys on the show.

After each week's episode was over, though, I returned to a harsh reality, where the drunk elephant was still passed out in Daddy's recliner.

Mamma told me that first night that it was time to go to sleep, but I couldn't sleep, literally and figuratively, that night or for many nights afterward. My weekly, one-hour *Kung Fu* reprieve—and the reruns that followed for years afterward—did not keep me or my family from diving into an abyss of insanity.

But it planted an important seed.

Honky-Tonk Heartbreak

MAMMA stood still in front of the dresser mirror, carefully leaning over a hot curling iron to get a closer image of her face. She gently rolled a brand-new stick of rich, candy-apple red lipstick over her modest lips. Mamma lightly pressed her lips together on a tissue, and then grabbed a bottle of perfume. She pressed her forefinger on the bottle opening, tipped the bottle once, then gently dabbed spots behind her ears and along her neck. Her preparation was an art form—a show I never tired of watching. When she wasn't looking, I grabbed the red lipstick-stained tissue and admired its curvy image.

From the living room, I heard the source of her motivation.

"Aaaa-yeee!" Daddy yelled at the TV. "I'm a pickin' and I'm a grinnin'. Hee-haw!"

From his chocolate-brown recliner, Daddy watched the country music TV variety show *Hee Haw*. He rose rather unsteadily from his chair and began a sloppy solo stomp polka around the living room.

As a five-year-old, I was too young to know the difference between days, but I knew my Saturday nights well.

"Put your jeans on," Mamma would say, handing me a pair of denim. My sisters, Nancy and Susan, waited excitedly on the couch. Daddy pulled on his boots at the kitchen table.

By 8:30 p.m., the family was dressed in our Sunday best for a Saturday night at a dance hall. I was already sleepy, for it was long past my bedtime. But it was Saturday night, and that meant that it would be many hours before I crawled into bed. Instead, I crawled into the backseat of the family's red station wagon, sitting on the

4

hard hump between Nancy and Susan.

We slowly rolled into the gravel parking lot of the corner liquor store. I see sawed between watching Mamma bite her lower lip and watching Daddy stumble into the store. Through the liquor store's glass window, I saw Daddy take the same route as last time. He knew exactly what he wanted and on which shelf it sat. Sometimes I would count to myself to see whether he moved faster or slower than the last time.

When buying liquor, Daddy was always efficient.

I sat in the backseat playing a guessing game: Which dance hall would we go to tonight? If Daddy turned left, we were bound for an old dive called The Corral. If he turned right, we were off to another shady dance hall called Mann's Hoe-Down, where the fiddle player was always drunk and the outdoor toilets housed a dry-heave-producing stench of beer piss and mothballs.

I hated the smell of Mann's Hoe-Down more than I loathed the icky men at The Corral, so I always hoped he'd turn left.

Daddy turned left.

To my young eyes, The Corral was a spooky cave, lit only by the glow of neon beer signs. Ace Williams and the Brazos Kings played loud country music onstage while bodies two-stepped and waltzed cheek-to-cheek on the sawdust-covered cement dance floor. Their movement provided the sole circulation to the thick, ghostly mass of cigarette smoke that hovered in the air like a winter fog. I didn't like The Corral. But I liked dancing with Daddy—before he got so hammered that his boots stomped all over my little toes. More than Daddy's stumbling, drunken polkas, though, I dreaded the moment that our dance was over because, back at my family's table, I'd inevitably feel a big hand touch my back shoulder. Behind me was always a huge, staggering, stubble-faced stranger asking me to dance. We were the only family in the joint, and we stood out. The men there were especially curious about and complimentary of me and my sisters.

"Ya got some fine-lookin' girls there, A.C.," the men would tell my dad. Daddy simply grinned and drunkenly nodded. Mamma bit her lower lip harder.

"Would you like to dance, little one?" they asked me.

My eyes pleaded for Daddy to say, "Get the hell away from my little girl, you goddamn pervert!" I didn't know what a pervert was then, but I knew there was something I didn't like about these men. Instead, Daddy always wore a proud, encouraging grin.

"Get after it!" he said approvingly.

Reluctantly, I took the big man's giant, callused, and sweaty hand and walked out onto The Corral's dance floor.

The men were all the same. Their eyes were bloodshot, their breath reeked of cigarettes and bourbon, and their shirts were dingy and drenched in sweat. My body was stiff, my movements rigid as we two-stepped. I didn't like them touching me, and I felt uncomfortable when they smiled and said I was "such a pretty young thang." After the dance, they always offered to buy me a soda pop. I accepted the offer because I thought that's what I was supposed to do, but I always returned to my family's table feeling like slimy boiled okra.

The only person at The Corral I liked was an old drunk named Cowboy. He used to be tall before alcoholism turned his posture into a perpetual slouch. He wore an old, dirty, beat-up straw hat and clothes that looked as if they had last been washed in the early 1900s. Cowboy would stagger from table to table; he stopped at ours to bullshit with Daddy and tell Mamma what beautiful girls she had. He never asked me to dance, so I liked him. We all politely smiled at Cowboy's drunken meanderings, and he eventually stumbled off to lean on someone else's table. Occasionally, Cowboy wouldn't show up on a Saturday night at The Corral, and everyone would knew why. Toward the end of the evening, the band passed the hat for the get-Cowboy-out-of-jail fund. The next week, Cowboy was back at The Corral, drunker than ever.

As Saturday night wore on, I fidgeted in a cold metal folding chair, rubbing my dry and itchy eyes from sleepiness and the ever-thickening honky-tonk smoke. The more I rubbed my eyes, the more they watered, and the more they watered, the more I felt the penetrating sting from the smoke. Tired and miserable, I vacillated between pestering the shit out of Mamma about when we were going home and watching Daddy pour more bourbon and less soda with every round of drinks.

"Mamma, is it time to go home yet?" I whined.

"Not yet," she said. We rarely left The Corral before midnight, and often stayed for the last song at 2 a.m.

I sat impatiently, watching everything and everyone. Whenever Daddy left the table, Mamma carefully lifted the bourbon bottle out of its tall, brown paper sack to see how much liquor was left. Her wrinkled brow and sigh signaled disapproval and disappointment.

"Mamma, is it time to go home now?" I said a few minutes later.

"Not yet," she said, putting two metal folding chairs together. "Here. Lie down."

The chairs were morgue-grade cold and uncomfortable, but eventually I fell asleep, awakened when it was time to leave. At first, I was sleepily relieved. Before we could get out of the bar, though, we'd have to make our way through a scary, narrow corridor. The Corral's owner was a tall, heavyset man with a permanent beer belly. He was perpetually pissed off at a small, stout bartender named Shorty. They got into a lot of arguments at closing time. One night, their verbal fight turned physical just as my family entered that cramped corridor. Trapped and terrified, I stood paralyzed amid the flying fists. I watched Daddy's eyes grow wild. His face turned red, not out of instinctual paternal protection of his wife and children, but rather because he wanted to jump into the brawl himself. Mamma calmly steered my sisters and me through the corridor and safely out the door. Daddy begrudgingly staggered out behind us, mumbling and slurring, ranting and raving about how "it's not right for a big guy to pick on a little shrimp." I was so relieved that we were out of danger. Relief was short-lived, though, because as we walked closer to our station wagon, Mamma's half-hearted, after-dance debate over the car keys ensued.

"Alvin, why don't you let me drive?" she pleaded rather innocently.

"Naaah, shith, I can thrive...hee hee...driiiive," Daddy giggled as he struggled to get the key in the car door. That door chronicled the history of his drunken journeys; the area around the lock was surrounded by silver streaks from all the times he missed the lock with his keys.

My stomach soured and tensed. Mamma pursed her lips; she yelled the least when she needed to the most, sighing as she held the backseat door open for us girls.

At the end of every dance night, Daddy climbed into the driver's seat, Mamma shook her head in silent frustration, and I sat in the middle of the backseat, leaning my forearms on the front seat to watch Daddy steer. As a sleepy five-year-old, I didn't fully understand the danger of our ride home. I thought that it was normal for Daddy to weave in and out of yellow lines on the highway, and I was excited that he had a lot of friends on the road. So many people honked at him. I'd wave at the honking cars and couldn't understand why no one waved back.

As I grew older, I thought only that Daddy was a bad driver, and that if I would just stay quiet in the back seat and not bother him, he would stay in his lane. By pre-adolescence, a horrifying realization emerged: Those honking horns were not friendly toots, but rather heart-jolting warnings. Daddy was in fact a dangerous man—a cocked and bourbon-loaded pistol holstered in the driver's seat of that red station wagon.

Near Miss

THE fire-engine red tow truck beeped a rhythmic song as it slowly backed Daddy's wrecked Volkswagen bug into our backyard. The top of the passenger side was now one with the floorboard. Sharp edges of freshly mangled metal reflected brightly in the morning sunlight, but there was nothing bright, happy, or invigorating about the sight.

I had ridden in that black VW with Daddy just last week, returning from one of our fishing trips.

That could have been me, I thought.

Long ago, I lost my little-girl adoration for my father. There was a time when Daddy and I were buddies. He would take me along to hang out at his buddy's auto parts store, we'd play catch in the front yard, I'd hand him tools as he worked on cars, and he'd lead me by the hand down the produce aisle of the grocery store sampling grapes until we were full. (I was too young to know that we were supposed to *pay* for those grapes.) I missed those times. I missed *our* time. I missed the man I used to love, the one who now was more in love with alcohol than all members of our family combined.

Though often disappointed and heartbroken, I kept trying to rekindle a connection with Daddy. One of the things we did together was fish.

We always left for fishing trips on the Guadalupe River before sunrise, when car doors clicked softly and voices whispered. One morning, Daddy and I drove in the dark to a nearby bait shop. The tires of his dented and scratched up car crunched against the gravel parking lot. A neon "Bait Here" sign sizzled and flickered.

Daddy always left the radio on for me while I waited in the car,

9

and I sat mesmerized by the lights of the power plant in the distance. The plant was electric and alive, yet serene. I stared until the lights blended into a candle-like flame, dancing before my eyes, listening to my prayers, absorbing my fears, leaving me still. It reminded me of the many candlelit temple scenes in *Kung Fu.*

Daddy opened the car door, and the plant became a plant again. I felt my spirit ebb and my defenses rise. I smelled the familiar odor of alcohol already.

"You ready?" Daddy asked me, smiling. He never smiled in the morning. I knew he had already put on his mask. I was used to his maniacal, curved lips. I was used to how my breath jerked, how my muscles tensed, how I felt as if I were underwater without scuba gear. I was used to it, but I never liked it.

On the riverbank, Daddy made his debut toss. The reel zipped and plopped the sinker and worm-baited hook into the still river. This was my favorite part of our trip. The silence. We each sat there, not moving, not talking. Life that early in the morning on the edge of the riverbank was so serene. Birds chirped sweetly. The river flowed calmly and effortlessly. The sole sound from humans was the occasional plop of our fishing-line sinkers hitting the water. Occasionally, I'd look around at the ground, hoping to spot a grasshopper nearby. I never did.

As the morning progressed, a familiar obsession erupted. Daddy tossed his fingers around the tackle box, making cover noise, hoping that I wouldn't hear the vacuum-sealed pop of the beer can he kept hidden. I always heard everything.

Our time together began to unravel. Daddy cussed his tangled reel. The more he drank, the less he fished. Daddy began talking away from me. His back was turned, but I still smelled the alcohol.

"I wanna go home now," I finally said. He obliged.

We were a block from home when Daddy suddenly punched the gas pedal to beat a yellow traffic light at a corner. The passenger side tires lifted from the ground and I screamed. I sat horrified, motionless, clutching the seat belt's shoulder strap like a security blanket. The wheels settled.

Daddy said nothing as he pulled into our driveway. I didn't say anything either. We each held our tongues for different reasons. The

10

moment the car settled to a complete stop, I bolted out and ran into the house. I found Mamma making pressed ham sandwiches in the kitchen.

"I don't care what you say," I told Mamma. "I'm never riding in a car with him when he's drinking again!"

Mamma, forever the argue-monger, stared at me, surprisingly silent. She never said a word. Instead, she gave an understanding nod.

DADDY'S alcoholism was the focus of a nightly ritual in which Mamma pointed out every one of his glaring defects. Regardless of the day's events, Mamma was mad. Bless her heart: Her forceful methods couldn't keep a stubborn man from filling his insides with bourbon. Still, she kept up the pressure. She had a PhD in screaming in frustration.

Life with a drinker had turned Mamma into an uptight woman with a venomous, switchblade tongue and an icy stare. At five-foot, five-inches with brown, wavy hair, she was mostly all bark, unless you count the time—in a high-blood-pressure, frustrated tantrum— she repeatedly pounded a fresh loaf of bread over my father's head until he slid out of his dinner table chair in drunken laughter.

Mamma was perpetually angry with Daddy, and sometimes his punishment washed over onto us kids. I intuitively played the role of a mini-ninja before I even knew such secret warriors existed, tip-toeing around the house so as not to be heard or seen, dodging the angry stomps of Mamma on her way to get the truth out of Daddy about what happened to his paycheck from the brake shop.

Daddy always staggered home at 6:15 p.m. with a quart of beer in his right hand and several swigs of hard liquor already swishing around an empty stomach.

"How yooooou?" he asked me with overpowering bourbon breath. His trademark scent of booze, motor oil, and sweat was nauseating. I loved him immensely, but I couldn't figure out how to sit next to him at the dinner table without vomiting.

For the next thirty minutes, Mamma screamed at Daddy, her cheeks glowing redder and hotter by the minute. The veins in her neck swelled. Daddy sat perpendicular to the dinner table, staring at the floor while balancing the quart of beer on his knee. He cuddled that booze as if his life depended on it, slurring one excuse after another until he hit his nightly jackpot and told Mamma whatever she wanted to hear about why he drank. Sometimes he wouldn't say anything, and I always wondered what he was thinking. Was he even listening? Maybe he was making a mental list of lures to add to his fishing tackle box. Maybe he thought that if he pretended not to listen, Mamma would shut up.

She never did.

Instead, she encouraged my sisters and me to join in on the Daddy-bashing. Being good girls, we faithfully obliged, and at that point, our family plunged into a vicious primal state.

"Look at your Daddy, girls," Mamma said. "Take a good look. He's nothing but a drunk."

We each took hateful little bites out of his spirit. Daddy was a weak sheep and we were the hungry, unmerciful pack of wolves, taking painful nips at his heels.

"You're pathetic," Mamma said.

"Yeah, Daddy," my sisters and I confirmed.

"You disgust me," Mamma said.

"Yeah, Daddy," my sisters and I repeated.

"I can't stand the sight of you," Mamma said.

"Yeah," my sisters and I chimed, and one night I added, "And I'm never gonna be like you."

Daddy clutched his booze and stared at the floor. He never responded. He just sat there in a very Zen-like manner—still and quiet, falling deeper into a lonely, bottomless pit of a private hell.

MY love for Daddy waned more and more with every drink he took. His drinking was getting worse, and Mamma was powerless to stop him. No matter how many pints and quarts of liquor she poured down the sink, Daddy always had another bottle hidden in the car. Mamma was long beyond discouraged and disheartened, yet she wasn't quite ready to throw in the towel on almost twenty years of marriage.

The breaking point came easier for me.

Early one Saturday evening, Mamma and I gathered in the living

12

room to watch *Hee Haw*. It was Daddy's favorite show. Oddly, Daddy wasn't home yet. No one had heard from him.

Hours passed.

No Daddy.

The sun set.

No Daddy.

I watched Mamma pace the floor, thinking her face couldn't get any redder without exploding. I was wrong.

About 8:30 p.m., the phone rang, and I watched and listened as Mamma said a few "Yes, sirs" and "I understands" and finally, "Well, is he all right?" I knew it was bad news.

When she hung up the phone, Mamma charged into my oldest sister's room, where Nancy was getting ready for her date. My sister Susan and I followed.

"You need to call that boy and tell him you can't go tonight," Mamma said. "And I need your paycheck."

"But Mamma!" Nancy cried.

"Girls, your Daddy swerved to avoid hitting a deer and rolled his VW. He's in a hospital in Jourdanton."

"Where's Jourdanton?" I asked.

"Just get your jacket," Mamma snapped. "We need to go right now."

Nancy protested the injustice of having to cancel a perfectly good date and turn over a week's worth of hard-earned money for what we all knew was Daddy's first official drunk-driving accident. It was bound to happen one day. We weren't happy about it, but at least, to our knowledge, he hadn't hurt anyone but himself.

I DIDN'T think you could pack that much tension into a VW station wagon. No one said a word on the hour-long trip to Jourdanton. Still, I kept my eye on the veins in Mamma's neck. She was like an oil well primed to blow. I just knew this was going to be the night that one of those veins popped, spewing blood out her ears.

Finally in Jourdanton, we speed-walked to the hospital's emergency room entrance. Everyone was on edge. I hoped Daddy was all right, but at the same time wished he was banged up enough to learn his lesson. As we stood by Mamma at a counter, the head nurse stepped up.

"My husband's been in an accident," Mamma began. She offered the nurse Daddy's name.

The nurse's face soured.

"Oh, *him*," she said with a disgusted sneer. She looked us up and down with eyes full of revulsion.

"He's not here. The police have already taken him to jail," she said, hand on hip.

I hung my head. Mamma was embarrassed and uncharacteristically apologetic. Nancy knew she was going to lose even more of her paycheck. Susan just cried.

Back in the car, Mamma's veins eased. She seemed deflated. I could tell we were both feeling ashamed.

Mamma revved up the car and took off down the road. Jourdanton was a small town; we found the jail easily.

"Wait here," Mamma said. But Nancy got out of the car anyway. She wasn't about to just hand over her paycheck without seeing what it bought.

"Thank God," I mumbled to myself, glad I wouldn't have to face another person as the obvious daughter of *him*.

As Susan and I sat in the car, I studied the jail from the outside. It was a tall, dark, eerie building. Strange sounds came out of the bar-covered windows. It looked alive—mean and evil. Bad people were in there. *My father* was in there.

I felt so sad.

After about half an hour, three people came out of the front of the building and walked toward our car. Daddy was staggering between Mamma and Nancy, his brand-new white shirt splattered with blood. Daddy fell into the front passenger seat. He smelled like he had fallen into a vat of bourbon. Other than that, he looked fine. Drunk, but fine.

I felt so angry.

Once on the road back to San Antonio, it was obvious we were going to have another silent, tense trip home. Daddy teetered between passing out and fiddling with the radio dials to find a good country music station. His upper body repeatedly fell uncontrollably into Mamma's lap. Mamma slapped him back.

"Stop it, damn you!"

Daddy finally passed out. Snoring in the front seat, his open mouth produced a steady stream of drool that landed on his blood-soaked shirt. I saw my father with grave and disturbing clarity. All the vision Daddy had was focused on the next drink. And this was my father? This was it?

I would have given anything to have a father like Master Po.

Every drop of idyllic, unconditional childhood admiration I had for him was amputated that night. It was painful to cut myself off, but it was better than the pain I'd suffer if I risked loving him any longer. I swore to never love him again and repeated the pledge that I'd never be like him.

A loud crash of heavy chains tossed into the tow truck's bay jolted me back to the present. The burly driver slowly lowered the crushed VW bug onto the ground in our backyard. I walked around to the passenger side of the car for a closer look at the crushed metal. A bolt ripped through my body like an epileptic seizure. If I had been with him, there was no way I would have survived.

That could have been me, I thought. *I sat right there just last week. That could have been me.*

The tow truck slowly rolled out of our yard, leaving behind mangled evidence of the insanity of alcoholism. Daddy took a Polaroid picture of the VW and stuck it in the family photo album. Every time I saw it, I swore I'd never be like him.

I was almost right.

Lonely and Alone

IN a simple room decorated by wall posters of singers Donnie and Marie Osmond and actress Farrah Fawcett, I studied schoolbooks and wrote short stories. As an honor-roll, bookworm nerd, I studied spelling lists and wrote parodies of popular songs. I thought Mamma and Daddy would be proud of me if I brought home all As. If they were, they rarely said so. They had other worries. Nancy was on the verge of dropping out of school. Susan was failing PE. I was the good girl making the good grades, not getting into trouble. They didn't have to worry about me, so they didn't. I felt invisible. I had recurring dreams of going out to dinner with my family and not having a place at the table.

Luckily, I intuitively knew and accepted that home wasn't the place where I'd get my self-esteem. I received the love and attention I needed at school, where I made stellar grades and good impressions on teachers. In academics, I found a safe, predictable place for perfection and control. Right answers were right and wrong answers were wrong. It was the black-and-white reality I sought to make sense of and give order to an otherwise chaotic home life, where emotions changed with the tick of a clock. And even though some classmates called me a brownnoser teacher's pet, and others taunted me with a Spanish slang pronunciation of my last name that meant "faggot," being at school bought me much-needed time away from home. So I took the brunt of my classmates' teasing. I smiled, swallowed the hard knots in my throat, and tried not to cry. After a while, I got along with my classmates the same way I stayed safe at home: I used a variation of ninja-like invisibility skills and silliness honed from watching *The Carol Burnett Show*.

ALL my self-esteem came from academics. I had zero social skills or beauty. Sports-wise, I still couldn't volley a ball, hoop a ball, or run with a ball. No matter. As I grew older, I deemed athletics to be a risky venture anyway—something that would make me look like a tomboy faggot.

At school, I was most comfortable hanging around teachers and fellow bookworms. At home, I was happiest alone. I felt especially lucky to stay behind while my family went grocery shopping. With everyone gone, the house was peaceful and quiet, and it gave me a chance to rummage through old cigar boxes in my parents' bedroom to search for the adoption papers I knew had to exist. This couldn't really be my family. Daddy and Mamma couldn't be my parents. Not feeling like I fit in at school was one thing. Not feeling like I belonged in my own family was another.

For a few obsessed years, I daydreamed about having a father like Master Po—a wise man I could talk to, ask questions of, look up to, and admire.

I never found a Master Po or those adoption papers. My family always returned home, and I returned to my room.

Though from my room I could still hear Mamma yelling at Daddy, I zoned out the arguing by turning up Captain & Tennille records on the turntable. I wished Mamma would be quiet like the Captain and that Daddy might smile like Toni Tennille, and not just when he was drinking. (His stupid, drunken grin had long worn my affections raw.) I adored the Captain & Tennille, and I think Mamma did, too. While she was always yelling at Nancy to turn down Peter Frampton on the stereo, I could play Captain & Tennille records as loud as my little turntable would go.

DADDY drank his way through my middle-school years, and just before I entered high school, he and Mamma divorced.

My mother was heartbroken, but for me, Daddy's departure was a relief. The house was finally quiet, Mamma's rage romps ceased, and I felt like I could breathe and relax.

One Sunday, Daddy took me out for our first post-divorce, father-daughter lunch. It went well until we left the restaurant and he stopped off at a convenience store to grab a quart of beer. I don't

know where the words came from, but I set a boundary.
  "No drinking when we're together," I said.
  He agreed.
  I didn't hear from him again for years.

The Quest to Belong

STUDYING in my room and writing short stories while listening to Captain & Tennille records paid off. When I graduated from high school, I walked across the stage with a diploma, honors, and a full, four-year academic scholarship to the Texas public college of my choice. In a matter of weeks, I went from working part-time measuring fabric and cutting keys at a five-and-dime store to being a full-time college student.

Apprehensive and afraid, I entered college in uncharted territory: Daddy quit school in the eighth grade. Mamma quit in the sixth. Nancy and Susan begrudgingly finished high school. Why would *I* make it through college? I was terrified my freshman year, yet determined to study as hard as I could to hang on to that scholarship. I wanted to be a writer so badly.

As a staff reporter for San Antonio College's student newspaper, *The Ranger*, I yearned to fit in with the cynical, intellectual, and politically opinionated crowd of journalist wannabes. My classmates were cool, and everyone drank. I swore that I'd never turn out like Daddy, but it was only a matter of time before I felt too stupid to sip my soda while my peers chugged their Lone Stars.

One night, the newspaper staff gathered at an old icehouse near campus to celebrate having published another week's edition. Before long, one of my classmates called out the usual question.

"Wanna beer?" he asked, with a brew already in his hand. "Oh, that's right. You don't *drink*," he smirked.

I sensed a dare, and I craved a friend.

"Sure, I'll try one," I said confidently.

My first beer was a Schlitz, and I hated the taste. But I *loved* the effects. No longer shy and self-conscious, I had courage. Uninhibited, I talked ninety miles an hour to anyone about anything and I didn't care what others thought of me. I finally felt like I fit in somewhere, that people liked me—that I was less of an awkward social klutz. It was like the moment young Caine was invited into the temple.

A whole new world emerged. Now I saw the possibility of having lots of friends. Heck, now I saw the possibility of having a date. Finally, I felt free.

That night, I got drunk for the first time, and then promptly drove home. At one point on the drive, I realized that I had just run a red light. At another point, I came to after sitting at a green light for God knows how long. I don't know how I got home without killing anyone, but I did.

It was the first time I drove drunk.

It wasn't the last.

TWO years later when I transferred to the University of Texas at Austin, I again felt the pang of insecurity, the awkwardness of socializing, and the desire to fit in. This time, I had fifteen co-op housemates to befriend. Most women in the co-op drank. Some smoked marijuana. Others snorted cocaine and took speed, ecstasy, and other drugs. I stepped up to the chemical buffet remarkably easily and was proud when I discovered a genetic ability to outdrink my housemates. A different type of self-esteem emerged as I saw my peers pass out or throw up from too much alcohol, while I remained standing.

Under the influence of chemicals, I had the guts to try new things and take risks like crashing fraternity parties and peeking in on gay bars. Popping speed helped me study for exams.

When I drank, though, I had poor judgment and no backbone. I went along with the crowd, like the time I joined my roommates in giving an inebriated Texas A&M University student a ride back to his hotel and then stole his clothes and cologne as a prank. We crashed parties and lured the best-looking men—their jealous girlfriends looking on—away to our co-op house.

The next day, my housemates said I had done things that I didn't remember, but it never occurred to me that I had a problem with alcohol or drugs. I wasn't like Daddy. I was a college student, and, after all, everyone drank in college. It was just a phase.

ON weekdays, I was a good student, studying hard and working part-time at a fast-food restaurant. On weekends, I got drunk or high. Before I knew it, two hangover-filled and marijuana-toking years rolled by and I was four months away from a degree in journalism.

Most of my drinking friends had graduated, so I planned to move off campus and share an apartment with two other girls. I missed my friends, but what spurred the latest restlessness, irritability, and depression was the end of my first romantic relationship—a short summer fling. For two months, I felt alive and in love. For months later, I wallowed in self-pity, thinking I'd never love again. I didn't talk about it to anyone. I just kept drinking. This time, though, I couldn't drink enough to feel euphoric. The high became elusive. Depression was as thick and heavy as a wet flannel blanket. Alcohol had stopped working, and I found myself one day sitting across from a campus therapist, who told me I needed group counseling with other adult children of alcoholics.

"I'm going through a breakup," I told the therapist. "I haven't seen my father in years. He has nothing to do with this."

The therapist jotted down an address on a sheet, ripped the paper free, and handed it to me.

"Just go," she said.

I attended group counseling as prescribed, fell asleep during every session, and eventually quit going and kept drinking.

Though I was an emotional mess, a little flame flickered as I peeked at the martial arts section in the university course guide. I was embarrassed to admit that I really wanted to try martial arts. I was afraid I'd look stupid, silly, or tomboyish. I could never be like Grasshopper or even the real, phenomenal Bruce Lee. Who was I kidding? I was a five-foot, two-inch chubby, wide-hipped, couch-potato nerd with a fear of breathing hard.

I was about to graduate, though. It was my last chance.

I took a risk.

The First Step in the Thousand-Mile Journey

THE varnished wooden floor felt cool on my bare feet. The old gym room on the UT campus was hot and musty. All my senses were alive. My jaw dropped, and there it remained. I finally made it. The gym looked nothing like a Shaolin Temple, and the class wasn't kung fu, but rather taekwondo. Still, you couldn't wipe the smile off my face.

I stood amid a sea of white-clad beginners. Men and women of all shapes and sizes donned the same white cotton uniform with fresh, stiff white belts wrapped around the waists. The *dobok*, Korean for "uniform," was awkward, loose, and baggy. I understood that the uniform needed to be roomy to stretch, kick, and punch in comfort, but when I glanced at myself in the mirror, I looked like a fat, puffy, baby seal.

As I stood around the mass of students mingling before class, I watched a paper-thin fellow gracefully glide into the room. He was long-legged with curly, light-brown locks, a mustache, and a mole on his day-old bearded cheek. Master Pliska was confident, stood straight and secure, and possessed a sharp gaze. At first, I was disappointed that he wasn't Asian. How could I learn martial arts from a white guy? Then I remembered: *Kung Fu* star David Carradine wasn't Asian either.

Master Pliska began the first class with a lecture about respect, order, and the value of working hard. I listened intently to most of what he said but was preoccupied with the fact that my white belt was so new and stiff that it stuck outward like an uncontrollable cowlick. I repeatedly yanked the two ends of the belt downward, but

22

they never fell gracefully to the side of each hip in the mustache-like, inverted V shape of Master Pliska's black belt.

"You over there," Master Pliska said to me. "Stop playing with your belt. Focus."

I nodded in acknowledgment.

"Yes, sir?" he said, coaching my reply.

"Oh. Yes, sir!" I said.

"That's better."

Soon the real work began, and I immediately fell in love. Years of walking on eggshells around Mamma and stuffing down my frustration over Daddy finally came out in a safe environment. The kicking, punching, and yelling I did in class was energizing and freeing. No one told me to shut up. I could shout awkward yet exhilarating spirit yells—Master Pliska called them *kihaps*—as loud as I wanted. I often didn't know what I was doing, turning left when the rest of the class faced right, and I couldn't understand one word of what Master Pliska said in Korean, but I was having a great time. The hour-long class ended too soon.

Master Pliska looked and acted nothing like Master Po, but he turned out to be a good teacher. He was demanding and tough, yet thorough and encouraging. He was a stickler for little details, a quality that as a copyediting apprentice I appreciated.

"I can see light coming through that hand of yours," he yelled to me one day from across the gym floor. "Tighten that fist!"

"Yes, sir!"

"Your front stance is too narrow," he barked another day, sweeping his ankle against mine. "Widen it!"

"Yes, sir!"

I learned the basic white belt techniques quickly, and suddenly taekwondo became an unexpected and vast source of confidence. I had stumbled onto something extraordinary. Taekwondo felt natural; it was physically challenging, yet comfortable, second-nature, exhilarating, and positive. Self-esteem exploded. The next class seemed like a vacation for which I couldn't wait. It was the first time that I had felt like I was good at something besides academics. Academics and writing were my first passions. Now I'd found another.

In the living room of my apartment, I spent evenings practicing kicks. My favorite technique was the knee kick. I loved hearing the crisp pop as my palms slapped my knee at the point of impact. A body-wide, tingling sensation rolled through my bones. I felt alive. When I practiced, I became focused, almost entranced. The most recent bout of depression had been replaced by a whirlwind of endorphins. I felt higher than any previous toke of marijuana. My ability to concentrate improved. Procrastination took a sabbatical. That semester, I wrote seven lengthy term papers and breezed through a hectic load of exams. I had endless energy. I even took up jogging, and the fact that I breathed heavily didn't make me think I'd die of a heart attack on a street corner.

I wondered if this is what happiness and serenity was like—what Grasshopper had really felt. Was this what I had been longing for, searching for, all these years? Whatever the martial arts were, I had found something special. I still thought the uniform made me look fat, but my confidence level was so high that I no longer cared. I was excited and wanted to share what I'd learned with the whole world.

I started with my family. That was my first mistake.

At home on Thanksgiving Day, I stood in the kitchen with Mamma, raving about this kick and that punch and how much I loved martial arts. She nodded periodically as she peeled spuds for a potato salad. "That's good," she occasionally said, never looking up from the salad bowl.

Mamma was distracted, but my brother-in-law Ed, who sat in the living room recliner, heard everything. Soon he began a bad-mouthing barrage against my newfound passion. At over six feet tall with a solid frame, Ed made his living working with his hands as a machinist at an air force base. He spent weekends tinkering with cars. He had a strong grip, but none of this mattered to me.

"Oh, bullshit!" he said, rising from the chair and walking into the kitchen. "That martial arts stuff ain't nothing."

"Oh yeah?" I said.

"Prove it," Ed dared, yanking up his loose-fitting Levi jeans by the belt loop.

I accepted his challenge.

That was my second mistake.

"O.K., grab my wrist," I said, planning to show him the wrist grab escape technique I learned in class that week.

"Like this?" he said, grabbing and twisting my left wrist with both hands. He torqued my wrist with such force that a sharp pain bolted up my arm. I tried the escape technique just as I learned it in class, but it wasn't working. The more I struggled to free my wrist, the more Ed twisted. My wrist, my entire arm, radiated with pain as I cried out in agony.

"Go ahead," Ed sinisterly giggled. "Show me something!"

I couldn't budge from his grasp. Instead of being the master of escape, I cried "uncle" in defeat.

"O.K. Let go!" I pleaded.

"Come on!" Ed said. "Show me how you're gonna get outta this. You said you could."

"Ed, let go. You're hurting me!"

Tears welled up in my eyes, but Ed wouldn't let go.

"Ed!" Mamma snapped, finally looking up from her potato salad. "Let her go!" she ordered, pointing a potato peeler at him. He finally released my wrist.

"See, I told you that martial arts stuff's a bunch of bullshit. And you're nothing but a big baby," Ed laughed, returning to the recliner and the Macy's Thanksgiving Day Parade on television.

I raced to the back room, hoping no one noticed the tears.

Which hurt more: the pain of Ed's strong, torquing grasp or the embarrassment of not being able to get out of a simple wrist grab? I felt like a fake. Then I felt angry, as if Master Pliska had betrayed me—duped me into believing that I could actually defend myself. Crying face down on my old bed, I began thinking that maybe this martial arts stuff really was just a bunch of crap, that *Kung Fu* and Bruce Lee movies were filled with fancy gimmicks and tricks.

All the confidence I'd built up was now crushed. *Kung Fu* was a Hollywood fantasy, and Grasshopper's serenity didn't exist outside a nineteen-inch TV world. There was no use searching for inner peace, confidence, or strength, for stronger people like Ed would always be there to beat me down.

AS the semester drew to a close, I continued attending taekwondo class regularly, albeit skeptically and apathetically. Embarrassed by the Thanksgiving Day fiasco, I muddled through the final days, regarding taekwondo as just an art class. The kicks and punches I learned now meant nothing more than a ballet star's pirouette, the patterns just an ice skater's figure eight. With renewed resignation came a deep sadness. I had lost my inspiration. The spirit of Master Po was dead, just like in the film. I wished I'd never invited Ed to grab my wrist, and at the same time I was grateful he did, for now I knew the truth. Martial arts wouldn't save me if I needed to defend myself, and it certainly wasn't the perfect path to peace that I'd hoped.

Master Pliska's final exam was quite easy. I punched and kicked hard and had good form.

"You've been doing real well," Master Pliska said after the test, rubbing his chin with his thumb and forefinger. "You're ready to test for your yellow belt now."

"Yes, sir," I replied.

"You can come to the Institute and take the test in December there."

"Thank you, sir," I said, bowing as I shook his hand. He only extended invitations to the off-campus Martial Arts Institute to serious students. Part of me felt proud and honored. Special. The other half sad. Chicken-shit cowardly. I knew I'd never show my face there. I had no intention of taking that test in December. What good is a yellow belt if I can't get out of a simple wrist grab?

Master Pliska wished me luck on my final exams, and I walked out of that old gym, through campus, and on to the bus stop in a sad, surreal daze. How could Master Pliska believe in me so much when I had lost all belief in myself? A familiar discouragement followed by the usual restless anxiety ensued, and I had to get away.

Turning my back on Master Pliska and taekwondo, I packed up and left town for my first newspaper job, skipping the Institute's December promotion exam and not even walking across the graduation stage with the rest of my university classmates.

I left behind the first of many unfinished tasks and self-sabotaged dreams.

Lost and Found

TURNS out coming from an alcoholic home can be good for a career in the high-pressure world of newspapers. I remained calm while covering gory car crashes, disturbing court cases, and high-profile drug busts. I went home alone and drank myself to sleep.

On the outside, I excelled. But on the inside, I was a ten-car pileup of emotions. My career path looped and zigzagged like a pre-schooler with an Etch-A-Sketch.

For the first few years out of college, I roamed from city to city and newspaper to newspaper, an actively drinking, spiritually sleep-walking zombie. No matter where I lived or worked, I was never happy for long, and I always moved on to the next geographic fix. Moving became the latest solution in the pursuit of happiness. The grass was always greener elsewhere. Anywhere. Each city offered the quick high of being in a new place and of the belief that this time I would be happy. After about six months, though, the newness always wore off. So I moved to another apartment. Eventually, the mythical greener grass always dulled to a brown, depressing hue. Reality set in that I still wasn't happy. I checked out library books on happiness to no avail. I picked up and moved again and again. In my first two years out of college, I worked for three different newspapers, hopping like a jackrabbit from East Texas to West Texas and finally ending up in South Texas along the Gulf of Mexico.

I moved so often that one day Mamma refused to write down my new phone number.

"I can't keep up," she sighed. "You can call me from now on."

I couldn't keep up the façade. I was a depressed drunk, again on the verge of another geographic fix to a newspaper job in San Antonio. I vowed to have a soda at my going-away party. By the end of the night, I was thoroughly intoxicated and, this time, downright snotty and belligerent. Booze gave me the courage to confront my boss.

"You're a real asshole," I said.

Luckily, my boss was just as drunk and didn't take me seriously. He laughed and slapped me on the back.

Next, I turned to a colleague who had just arrived. I slurred and spit as I talked a mile a minute about nothing. He looked me up and down.

"Man, you're drunk," he said with disgust.

His words sobered me immediately, and I felt hurt and ashamed. *How did I end up drunk again?*

I stumbled and staggered out of that Corpus Christi bar, and as I tried to force the key into the driver's side lock, I realized a truth.

Shit. I'm just like Daddy.

In a split second, life fast-forwarded to me losing my career, money, family, freedom, and sanity. Daddy's drinking didn't escalate until his mid-forties. I was 27. I knew that I had a head start on him, and if I continued I was destined to die a frail, wet-brained shell of a person from cirrhosis of the liver.

Without thinking, I uttered a prayer:

Oh, God, please help me. I can't do this anymore.

The next day, I awoke with another hangover, yet something seemed different. I felt an uneasy calm—uneasy more because it was unfamiliar and unpredictable. There was no time to analyze it, though. The moving van was due in a few hours.

LIFE was neither sane nor serene in San Antonio. A few white-knuckled months later, I dragged myself to my first sober meeting. I snuck into a club on a Thursday morning, but I must have had a deer-in-the-headlights look because a woman immediately greeted me in the lobby.

"Hi, honey," she said. "I'm Gracie. You're new, aren't you?"

I nodded.

"Well, let me buy you a cup of coffee," she said, grabbing my arm, leading me to a coffee bar in the corner of the room.

"That's O.K.," I defiantly replied, pulling away. "I can buy my own coffee."

I may be a drunk, but I'm not a bum!

"No, honey," she snapped back. "This is how it works around here: I buy you a cup of coffee, and then you buy another new person a cup of coffee someday."

She grabbed my arm again and led me to the coffee bar. Gracie was a persistent little booger. Tall with wild, dark-brown hair, she had big teeth and wore thick makeup—everywhere. It was hard to tell her age, but her face looked as if she'd lived a hard life.

"Here you go," she said, handing me a cup. "Come with me. The meeting's down this hall."

Gracie led me back to a small room at the end of a long corridor.

"You can sit here," she said, pointing toward a chair by the door. "My chair's up there."

Gracie hobbled down the aisle and took a seat at a desk in the front of the room.

She opened the meeting and began swearing like a sailor.

Fuck, fuck, fuckety-fuck.

I almost spit out my coffee in shock and amusement. It wasn't what I expected at a sober meeting. I imagined that sober people were a depressed lot who spent their lives moaning and crying about not being able to drink anymore.

This was intriguing; I stayed.

Gracie opened the meeting by asking everyone to introduce themselves. The first woman said, "Hi, I'm Betty, and I'm an alcoholic."

I panicked and thought about bolting from the room. I couldn't tell everyone I was an alcoholic. Then they'd *know*.

As the women continued their introductions, though, it occurred to me that they were *all* alcoholics, too. I don't know where I found the courage, but when it came to my turn, I said for the first time: "I'm Cathy, and I'm an alcoholic."

"Hi, Cathy," the entire room responded, washing me in a wave of compassion and love. It was as if everyone there had been waiting for me to come and to say those words. They all smiled at me and seemed truly glad I was there.

I stayed.

The rest of the meeting was a blur, but I remember feeling comforted, so I went back the next day, and every day after that. I wasn't happy about being an alcoholic—that I had become the very thing I loathed as a child. Still, the knowledge somehow made life a little more bearable, which I needed because I was drowning in a sea of insecurity at my job. Always the big fish in the small newspaper pond, I was now treated as an annoying batboy in journalism's major league, working amid the nastiest newspaper war in the state. Grumpy editors were always on my ass for being too slow or too careful.

"Cathy, I don't need a fucking analysis of that drive-by shooting," the copy chief snapped. "Turn it loose!"

Every night, I went home in tears. Little white sores formed on the top of my mouth and I was convinced I had AIDS and was going to die. Every night at a makeshift prayer table, I sat cross-legged on the dull-brown carpeted floor of my townhouse, weeping and pleading for help from the Universe. I didn't think anyone heard me, and I wasn't even sure who or what I was praying to, but I kept praying anyway because that's what the folks in my sober meetings told me to do.

When I wasn't working or crying, I went to meetings, but I was too ashamed to get a mentor to help guide me in sobriety. I couldn't bear to share my secrets with another person. So I sat at my kitchen table one night and decided to work the recommended twelve steps myself. I started with the recommendation to make "a searching and fearless moral inventory of ourselves."

I wrote down all my defects.

I'm a really bad daughter and sister.

I don't call for months at a time, and I forget birthdays.

I'm a perfectionist and a horrible procrastinator.

If I don't think I can do something perfectly, I put it off, and often don't try at all.

There was one nagging secret I was afraid to write down. It wasn't that I never knew it about myself. I just wished it would go away one day. I hoped that if I prayed enough or prayed the right way, this defect would be removed. But it was still there. Been there since I could remember. I swallowed hard and wrote it down:

I'm gay.

I felt the bottom fall out of my stomach. That summer fling in college with another woman was no fling. The longer I sat looking at those two words, the more memories emerged.

My first crush was on a girl in the fifth grade. She was tall with long blonde hair, and I thought she hung the moon. She was a class-mate, but she wasn't necessarily my friend. I was too shy to have friends. I just quietly admired her from afar as she ran around the playground in her pretty dress and beautiful hair.

Having crushes on other women was common for me, but I rarely did anything about these infatuations. Sitting at the kitchen table remembering all the women I'd been attracted to over the years, I realized that my most common crushes were on straight, married women. They were safe; I knew nothing would come of those relationships.

Confused and in pain, I didn't want to accept being gay because of all the shit I feared I'd get from society—and Mamma. But I knew the truth.

I cried myself to sleep.

THE women in the sober meetings often said that secrets keep us sick. I wanted desperately to stay sober, so the next day I decided to get a sponsor. After a meeting one morning, I begrudgingly walked up to a pudgy, short, dark-haired Hispanic woman and asked her to be my sponsor. Hilda C. always sat in the front row with a crew of blue-haired Baptist ladies and talked openly about her partner, Sheryl. To my shock, when I asked Hilda to be my sponsor, she didn't immediately say yes. Instead, she invited me over to her house for "lesbian coffee"—Folgers with a dash of cinnamon. As we sat on her sofa, she asked me about why I had come to the meetings, and I searched for a sane manner in which to tell her I was crazy, gay, and would probably die soon.

She remained deadpan.

"You know, there's probably nothing you can tell me about

yourself and your past that I haven't heard before. You're a sick alcoholic. None of us comes here because we're well."

Her frankness was stunning.

"I'll work with you," she finally said, "but here are the conditions: I won't bail you out of jail. I won't lend you money. I won't sleep with you. You can't stay at my house. And you have to get out of your self-pity. Be of service to others: Make coffee before meetings, empty ashtrays after meetings. Your job right now is to not drink. Seek God, clean house, and help others."

I had no problem cleaning my apartment or helping old ladies cross the street. But I didn't want to seek God too hard because I was pretty sure he didn't like me. My parents never took me to church, and Grandma told me as a child that God was sending my sisters and me on a one-way bullet train to hell because Mamma and Daddy didn't get married in a Catholic church.

"Do I have to go to church?" I asked Hilda.

She made it clear: We weren't talking about church; we were talking about God.

As my eyes drifted around Hilda's quiet, neat, sage-scented living room, and as I sipped coffee, I realized she had something I wanted: serenity. She was like Master Po, only in a Hispanic female body.

For the next six months, I met Hilda at her house once a week to read through a sober text called the *Big Book* and to work the steps toward recovery. The more I worked with Hilda, the more her peaceful aura rubbed off. But we butted heads over her prodding me to seek a Higher Power, as the program suggests. I balked.

"You just need to start looking for God," Hilda insisted, "because He's everywhere, and He loves you."

I rolled my eyes.

She sighed, then gave me homework.

"Every time you see one of those fish decals on cars or any type of spiritual bumper sticker, say out loud, 'There's God.'"

"Fish?" I asked. "What fish are you talking about? Like bass?"

"This," Hilda said, grabbing a pen and paper and drawing a kindergarten-grade, stick-figure fish.

"O.K." I said skeptically. "Never seen it before."

"You will," Hilda said confidently. "Just open your eyes. Look for God. He's there. You just have to look."

The next day on my way to work, it was as if everyone and their grandmother had put those stupid stick-figure fish on their cars overnight.

Fish were everywhere. Fish-decaled cars haphazardly wove into my lane and suddenly slammed on their brakes in front of me on the highway.

There's God, I thought.

A loud, beat-up Pinto passed me on the road; it had a fish decal.

There's God—and He needs a new muffler.

A frozen food truck with the word "FISH" in big letters passed.

Very funny, God.

I'd never seen these fish before.

Now they were everywhere.

I was waking up.

SPOTTING fish became a game. The timing of the sightings was eerily comforting. When I was having a bad day, I'd see a fish decal and immediately feel better. When I needed to make a decision and knew in my gut what I needed to do, I'd see a fish and feel validated.

My heart was opening, and although I knew it was good for me, it was painful. I cried every night at my prayer table. I feared I was depressed again.

"When's the last time you cried?" Hilda asked one day. "Presobriety?"

I immediately knew the answer.

"I was nine when Mamma made me lie on Nancy's bed while she whipped me with a leather belt. I don't remember why I got a whipping, but I remember it wasn't my fault. I decided then that I wouldn't give her the satisfaction of seeing me cry. I haven't cried since."

Hilda nodded understandingly.

"Then you've got a lot of crying to catch up with," she said.

Pulling away from Hilda's house that night, I saw a fish decal on a car at the corner stop sign.

I bawled little-girl tears all the way home.

Cathy Chapaty

Part II

The Kyoshi Era

Cathy Chapaty

The Man with Popeye Arms

S OBER one year, I celebrated by treating myself to a movie. As I exited the mall cinema, I heard a startling, queer noise echoing down a corridor of clothing, beauty, and shoe shops. I followed the noise and spotted a small crowd of people gazing into a storefront window.

Then I heard the noise again.

It sounded like a sharp chant: loud, crisp, rhythmic, and methodical. It was coming from inside the last shop on the right.

When I finally nudged my way through the crowd, I saw the little people making all that big noise. It was a karate school, packed with children yelling thunderous *kihaps* as they kicked. They were all so cute in their little white karate uniforms and little white, yellow, orange, green, and blue belts. They had little feet and little hands, and all smiled wide grins as they kicked, punched, jumped, and rolled. I grinned too as I surveyed the class, remembering how much fun I had taking taekwondo with Master Pliska at the University of Texas.

Then, out of the corner of my eye, I saw *him*. He was not a big man physically, yet he carried a large, distinguished presence in his black kung fu uniform. Standing barefoot on a spotless wooden floor, he had a shiny bald head, a finely trimmed goatee, and huge forearms to rival the cartoon character Popeye. His deep, hearty laugh was both startling and contagious. Staring at him in awe, I walked into the school and sat down on the spectator benches.

I didn't quite understand where he'd come from. I'd been in that mall many times before and had never seen him or the school. Yet there they were, and I felt drawn to him.

37

As I watched the class, I remembered Hilda's most recent words. We were deep into our step work, now at the point in which I needed to begin making amends for past wrongs.

"Don't forget to include yourself on that list," she said.

In our work, Hilda helped me unpack a lot of regrets, and one of those regrets was leaving Austin without taking Master Pliska's taekwondo test.

My heart raced as I walked into the office to inquire about classes. In a cramped room, a young woman with reddish-brown permed hair and perfect makeup sat behind a desk, waiting almost expectantly.

I didn't need her to sell me on the school's program. I signed up immediately, and as I delivered my indistinguishable signature for the school's beginner program, I felt a strange combination of excitement and serenity.

I had not found Master Po in the mall that day.

I found Kyoshi, and I immediately adored and worshipped him.

ON the first day of class, I wore my old taekwondo uniform from college. Thrilled that it still fit, I felt strong and empowered again, and I decided that I wouldn't quit until I got a yellow belt and finished what I started with Master Pliska.

Kyoshi ordered the class to line up. We bowed to Kyoshi. He began a light joint warm-up. I studied him. Kyoshi's movements were mesmerizing, powerful, and graceful. I marveled at his defined muscular build made of finely cut pecs and bulging forearms. I fell in love with his loud laugh and his quizzical facial expressions. I trusted him immediately and completely and was willing to go to any lengths requested—until he gave the order to run laps around the dojo. Anxiety set in. I hoped I wouldn't drop dead in front of my new instructor. That would be so embarrassing.

Kyoshi took off in a quick sprint circling the dojo's hardwood floor. He seemed to fly. So did all my classmates. As the newest student, I was at the back of the heap, already panting heavily though the class had only completed Lap Two. Panic mounted. I was sure I'd have a heart attack.

Oh, God, please help me through this, I silently prayed while panting. *I don't remember having to run in Master Pliska's class.*

My mind's negative chatter wouldn't cease.

With Kyoshi in the lead, we ran. And we ran. And we ran some more. When we finally stopped, I whispered an exhausted, breathless thanks to whatever spiritual entity might be listening.

Next the class sardined together at a ballet barre on which we each rested one leg, toes to the ceiling, and stretched our torsos forward. I felt awkward and was suddenly conscious of a male shopper gawking at my crotch through the studio window.

We then began some light kicking drills, and I began to relax. It was all starting to come back to me now: front kick, side kick, roundhouse kick. I knew them all, and Kyoshi seemed impressed. He didn't know that I'd taken taekwondo in college. I was happy that he was happy, and I was so pleased to please him that I didn't pay attention to his next command. Suddenly, the class followed Kyoshi to the back of the studio, where he pulled out and unfolded a long, royal-blue, two-inch-thick cushioned mat. My classmates knew exactly what to do, for as soon as the mat was flat on the floor, like assembly-line dominoes, they rolled head over heels one after another. When they got to the end of the mat, they recovered and quickly trotted around to the beginning of the mat and rolled again.

I watched in terror.

I don't remember rolling in Master Pliska's class.

This looks dangerous.

I could break my neck.

He's not going to expect me to do this on my first day, is he?

Yes, he was.

I lined up to the edge of the mat, hesitant and afraid. I didn't want to snap my neck and become paralyzed for the rest of my life just for a stupid yellow belt. Kyoshi must have sensed my reluctance, for he showed me step by step how to do a forward roll. I tried following his instructions but felt like I was a three-year-old doing a cartwheel for the first time: slow, uncoordinated, and flat. There was no roll to it. I fell over with a thud.

"Do it again," Kyoshi ordered.

I rolled once more, this time with ease.

"That's right!" Kyoshi exclaimed. "You got it! See, gravity will do it for you."

I rolled again and again until I became dizzy and disoriented and bopped my head on the mat.

Kyoshi's upside-down image came into view as I lay flat on my back like a defenseless doodlebug.

"Don't hit your head," Kyoshi said, hands on his hips. "Look at your belt when you roll and tuck your head. You gotta tuck your head!"

"Yes, sir!" I said, jumping up to avoid the other students whisking past me as they rolled, recovered, rolled, and recovered. They obviously had been monkeys in a previous life.

My classmates made it look so easy. But if rolling was so easy, why did my head hurt?

I searched for a clock, wondering when the class would end. Kyoshi, meanwhile, searched for the first guinea pig for the Medicine Ball Drill, in which one student at a time stood in the corner of two walls and avoided a heavy, bulky medicine ball hurled at them at increasing speed. I watched in horror and shock as my classmates put the previous drill to practical use, rolling out of the way of the careening ball and quickly recovering before Kyoshi threw the ball again.

"Better roll out of the way, or you're gonna get hit," Kyoshi said. "Here it comes again."

Bam!

Kyoshi slammed the ball against the wall.

Bam!

He was merciless.

Bam!

"Move!" he barked. "You gotta move!"

Kyoshi threw the ball faster and harder. My classmates looked like human pinballs: dodging, rolling, and recovering; dodging, rolling, and recovering. When the students tired, Kyoshi eventually nicked them with the ball. Anxiously awaiting my turn, I felt neither prepared nor particularly happy about the probability of getting smacked with that ball just for a stupid yellow belt.

Luckily, the class ended before my turn.

I released a huge sigh.

My first martial arts class in six years wasn't the effortless, easy experience I remembered from college. But it was something I could imagine Grasshopper doing at a Shaolin Temple, so I was willing to return.

Kyoshi eventually called the class together in the spot where we originally began, and I heard for the first time a mantra that would make an imprint on my heart forever: the school's student creed.

We must be gentle and kind,
But ferocious in combat.
We must be respectful toward others:
Superior or inferior, friend or foe.
We must love what is good and just,
And shun what is evil.
We will abide in gentleness, respect, and Agape love.

And that's when I knew it:
I was home.

Let's Go for the Mark

TIGER Balm is like gold to a martial artist. I dug my fingers into the tiny bottle's yellow ointment and rubbed that stuff over muscles I didn't even realize I had before I began training with Kyoshi. My shoulders ached from push-ups and the pull-ups and hanging drills on the school's monkey bars. My forearms were freckled with bruises from practicing hand-to-hand blocks, and the balls of my feet bore painful, tender blisters from pivoting and sliding on the hardwood floor. In the beginning, training was uncomfortable, and I thought I might just be a masochist. In time, my muscles strengthened, my feet toughened to form a layer of calluses, and self-esteem improved, too.

Every day, I also learned a little more about Kyoshi. The mere sight of him struck me with awe, even though his confidence and flamboyance looked nothing like Master Po.

I'd suit up early, sitting on the spectator bench before class to watch Kyoshi train alone. If I was lucky, I caught him twirling and whisking around a long, thin stick called a *bo* while performing a graceful and fluid form. His strikes were quick and powerful; the *bo* sounded like a rotating helicopter blade. Kyoshi was especially mesmerizing when he trained with two silver rings, one around each forearm. He performed a beautiful form, moving slowly, gently, and gracefully forward, backward, and around like Gulf of Mexico waters lapping gently against the Corpus Christi shore.

My favorite form was a choreographed fighting sequence called "Heaven's Manna," a mesmerizing work of art demonstrating flexed forearms, fingers in tight snake-head formation, and unshakable balance. Kyoshi grunted and growled, stomped and glided with both

42

intensity and grace. I watched in awe, hoping he would teach Heaven's Manna to me one day.

Kyoshi was physically amazing, but I was most intrigued by a strong, captivating spirit. He'd spent ten years as a Buddhist monk, then after the death of his mother, he became a born-again Christian. I'd read about the occasional prison inmate who claimed to have been reborn, but I was skeptical that these conversions were genuine. On the scale of spiritual transformations, though, going from ten years as a Buddhist monk to life as a fundamentalist Christian was quite a leap of faith. Kyoshi's spiritual journey fascinated me. I wanted to know more. I wanted what he had.

At the end of my one-month trial, Kyoshi called me into his office to discuss my future training options. I was so nervous, I thought I'd faint. As I waited for him to get settled, my eyes roamed the room. He had a neatly kept bookshelf, a bust of Abraham Lincoln on a pedestal, and a paperweight placard that read "My Boss Is a Jewish Carpenter."

Kyoshi showed me an old photograph of him and a young woman training side by side. She was one of his first students, and he took her all the way to black belt.

"She came to me as a child, though. I haven't had a grown woman go from white to black yet," Kyoshi said, pausing. "I think you'd be a good candidate for that challenge."

A challenge.

Sounded like hard work.

"So you're ready to do this thing?" he asked, raising a thick left eyebrow as he leaned back in his chair. "You're ready to go for that black belt?"

"Yes, sir, I am," I lied, not sure I was ready at all. I hadn't even gotten my yellow belt. And that's all I came for. I knew I was no Grasshopper. I still felt the sting of the Thanksgiving Day fiasco. But I really liked this man. I wanted more. Though uncertain and afraid, I also felt the familiar pull that had led me to his karate studio in the first place.

Purely on faith, I penned another indistinguishable signature on a two-year contract and wrote out a whopper of a check to cover my tuition. We shook hands, and I physically felt for the first time the magnitude of Kyoshi's powerful yet gentle hands.

A few weeks later, a card arrived in the mail:

Let's go for the mark.
You've got what it takes.
Let's go for it!
Best,
Kyoshi

Tears trailed down my face. He probably sent thank-you cards to everyone who signed a contract. He had no idea how much just reading the words "You've got what it takes" meant to me. So I vowed to go for "the mark"—whatever that meant—because I wasn't ready to let go of my Grasshopper dream just yet.

Stretch

PERSEVERANCE is a funny thing—an element I never thought I possessed. That stuff was for Olympians and marathoners and people who didn't mind sweating a lot. I still walked around with a load of fear in my belly. I didn't see myself in that realm. Still, no matter how physically hard, mentally difficult, and spiritually trying training became, I showed up for class three days a week like clockwork. I kept trying—partly because of an ever-increasing admiration for Kyoshi and a growing bond with my classmates, and partly because of a big sign that hung toward the back of the dojo that in huge letters simply read "Don't Quit."

It reminded me of a key saying in sober meetings: "Keep coming back."

Every time I thought I couldn't run one more lap or pump out one more push-up, sit-up, kick, or punch, my tired eyes met that sign. Those two words kept me going when I didn't think I could go any farther. It proved me wrong more times than not. It infuriated me. Each time I thought I had reached my physical limit, I caught a glimpse of that sign, sighed, tried again, and somehow found the strength to complete whatever crazy drill Kyoshi ordered. Training was always like that with Kyoshi. He pushed me to my limits to prove how far I could really go. I always went farther than I imagined, and he intuitively knew when to stop pushing.

His favorite way of pushing the limit came in stretching, particularly in doing forward splits. One Monday, Kyoshi gathered the small noon class around an odd, archaic-looking contraption that my classmates called the Torture Machine. It was a gray, V-shaped metal apparatus with a padded seat in the center and a manual crank directly in front of the seated person's crotch. One by one, my class-mates climbed onto the machine and grimaced, moaned, and groaned as Kyoshi cranked the machine—and their legs—ever wider. From the pained expressions on their faces, my classmates each looked like they would divulge the secrets of the universe if they knew them just so Kyoshi would stop cranking that lever.

Still the last one to do anything in class, I braced for my turn. With a deep breath, I climbed on as if I were an urban cowboy and the Torture Machine a mechanical bull.

"Relax," Kyoshi reminded me. "Breathe. If you relax and breathe, you'll be amazed at how far you can stretch. If you resist, it's gonna hurt."

I relaxed as best I could as Kyoshi cranked the lever.

Squeak, squeak, squeak.

The 45-degree angle slowly grew to 60, 70, and then 90 degrees.

Squeak, squeak, squeak.

The gap between my legs widened to 100 degrees, then 120, 140, and 150. I was in pain.

"Breathe," Kyoshi said as he continued cranking.

Squeak, squeak, squeak.

"Oh, God!" I cried. "I'm gonna break!"

"You're not going to break. You're doing great," Kyoshi countered. "A little more. You can do it. Tell your mind to tell your muscles to relax."

The dial on the machine read 156, 158, 160. I didn't want to look anymore. My lower body felt like a dried-up wishbone. I was sure any moment I'd hear a loud snap and be broken in two. Then that's when it happened again.

My eyes met that damn sign: *Don't Quit.*

Crap!

I tried to relax. I put all my trust in Kyoshi—that he knew before I even sat down on this machine how far I could go. I sucked in and released deep breaths, and closed my eyes.

"There it is: 165!" Kyoshi cried, patting me on the shoulders. "That's enough for today, Miss Chapaty. See, I told you that you could do it. That's great for the first time!"

"Thank you, sir," I sighed, as Kyoshi loosened the crank enough for me to slowly ease out of the stretch. I rose to my feet and hobbled off in awkward tenderness, shaking my head and mumbling to myself.

... and I'm paying good money for this.

Yellow Is the New Black

THERE were many days early on in Kyoshi's dojo that I was sure I'd die from running laps during warm-up. Or during kicking drills. Or during rolling and falling practice. Instead, I grew stronger and continued to train harder. Finally, Kyoshi tapped me to test for the coveted yellow belt.

On an August evening, I held hands with Kyoshi's wife, Terri, in the women's dressing room while she said a quick prayer.

"Jesus, I just pray that you bless us with your heavenly strength," she said, squeezing both my hands. "Lord, help us through the next few hours and protect us from harm and injuries. Bless us with your grace and your glory. In your name we pray, Amen."

Good thing she said the part about protecting us from harm, because during the test I propelled myself right into a head-on collision with a shoulder-rolling black belt. I smacked into him like a cue ball on a pool table. Luckily, both of us walked away without a scratch and with our senses intact.

Though the thought of taking the test terrified me, in the end, the exam felt relatively easy.

A few hours later, I tore off my dirty white belt and Kyoshi wrapped a stiff, vibrant yellow belt around my waist. It had taken me six years since my last class with Master Pliska, but I finally got it, receiving solid marks and scoring highest in the areas of kata (or patterns) and character development. Only Terri scored higher.

That night I vowed to keep training—and outscore Terri next time.

"Can't" Gets You Fifty Push-ups

LESSONS in perseverance are plentiful in martial arts. I learned a lot from Kyoshi and that damn Don't Quit sign, but I'll never forget the spirit of Little Eddie, a student in the family class.

Eddie was practicing a technically demanding and dynamic form when Kyoshi stopped to coach him. Eddie was having trouble recovering from a roll with his bo and then leaping into a jump front kick. I didn't hear exactly what Kyoshi said. I just remember hearing Eddie—a small-for-his-age, clean-cut, sweet and kind nine-year-old—say, "I can't."

The previously noisy dojo became still and quiet. All eyes shifted to Kyoshi, then to Eddie, who finally realized his error, then back to Kyoshi, who looked dumbfounded.

In our dojo, the word "can't" was considered blasphemy. If spoken in Kyoshi's presence, it was punishable by fifty push-ups.

"What was that you said?" Kyoshi asked, his left eyebrow darting up sharply in disbelief. "Son, you couldn't have said what I thought you said."

Eddie remained quiet, safe for the moment.

Kyoshi, meanwhile, repeated his earlier instructions.

"But, sir, I've tried and I can't," Eddie said again.

Classmates gasped.

Kyoshi's going to kill him, I thought.

Kyoshi shook his head slowly and then ordered, "O.K., son, give me fifty push-ups right here."

"Fifty?" Eddie shot back, his at-ease military stance wavering. "Umm, sir, I can't do fifty push-ups altogether."

Nooooo!

49

"O.K., Mr. Martinez," Kyoshi said. All students knew that when Kyoshi addressed you as Mr. Anything after previously addressing you as "son," you were in big trouble. "Then give me one hundred."

Kyoshi's arms were now folded, both eyebrows raised, and his face flat and serious.

Little Eddie fell to the floor, and with only his hands and balls of feet touching the hardwood floor began pumping out push-ups. Everyone else resumed their training, but I watched Eddie in amazement. I didn't think I could do fifty push-ups either, definitely not one hundred, but I became inspired the longer I watched Eddie prove himself wrong. He completed every one of those push-ups as requested and rose to his feet. The room again became quiet.

"So, son, are you ready to continue?" Kyoshi said.

"Yes, sir!" Eddie shouted in confidence.

"Remember, son, do the best you can."

"Yes, sir," Eddie said.

That night, I bowed off the floor vowing to keep my mouth shut during class regarding what I thought I could or couldn't do. Years before the popular Nike advertising campaign, I learned from Kyoshi, Little Eddie, and that damned Don't Quit sign to "just do it."

Moving Up, Waking Up

WHEN the newspaper I worked for closed, I suddenly had a nice severance package, immediate unemployment benefits, and nothing better to do with my time but fill out job applications and train with Kyoshi. I threw myself into karate, and suddenly I was the one helping hesitant white belts learn how to roll and fall safely. Now I had time to help mentor the younger students and comfort the occasional crying five-year-old who thought his older classmates were shouting "KILL!" instead of strong *kihaps*.

No longer having to work nights and weekends at the newspaper was a gift, allowing me to compete in karate tournaments on Saturdays all over Texas. Training, and life in general, was better than ever, and I discovered through the tournament circuit a knack for forms. I regularly placed first and second in contests, my first trophy standing as tall as my nose. I was having a great time and learning a lot.

Attentive to every detail, Kyoshi insisted on clean technique, hard punches, crisp knife-hands, and solid, uniform-snapping kicks.

"Kick harder!" Kyoshi ordered. "You want to knock your opponent into next week."

Kyoshi loved deep, solid stances. My quadriceps cried every time he led the class in a low-crouching cat stance drill. Sometimes he'd order us to sit in a deep horse stance and then leave us there for minutes at a time while he went into the office to make a phone call. My muscles were so regularly fatigued that my legs and arms shook on the car ride home. On Thursday nights, Kyoshi preached about quick sparring reflexes and undying endurance.

"Miss Chapaty, you need to start running," he advised. "That's the only way you're gonna build endurance. If not, you're gonna die out there."

There were moments during sparring when I thought I *had* died and gone to heaven, until I realized that the angelic voices wafting through the air while I was getting my butt kicked were from the church next door, where the Daystar Church choir practiced songs for its Sunday service.

AS a radiant orange belt, I trained often and was happy, a rarity in my depression-laden past. I especially liked kicking drills we performed using old X-ray sheets. The X-ray sheets made a cool, shattering, popping noise every time I hit the target dead center. Flexibility was improving, and although my legs still didn't split all the way down to the floor, I was regularly holding a 160-degree stretch without the aid of the Torture Machine. My strides seemingly weren't good enough for Kyoshi, though. He always pushed for more and better, and he invited me to test for the next rank.

"I don't know, sir," I said. "I don't think I'm ready."

"Oh, you're ready all right," he said loudly, letting out a hearty laugh. "You just need to commit."

"O.K., sir. I'll try."

"Don't try. Do," he said as his eyebrows leveled. I knew he was serious.

Commitment. One of Kyoshi's favorite words. Kyoshi was always preaching about goals. I was unemployed. I had no goals. And I didn't want any, either. I was at ease amid complacency and had no desire to push the envelope to see how much farther I could excel because I was scared. Yet there was Kyoshi, my idol and mentor, telling me to set a goal and take a risk, regardless of whether I thought I could succeed. It was just another way of saying, "Don't Quit."

True to my promise on that first day of class, I trusted Kyoshi's judgment and did what he recommended. I finally took the test for green belt.

Though in the two prior tests I had excelled, this time I made a lot of simple mistakes, and if I hadn't spent so much time mentally beating up on myself, I might not have gotten so physically beaten up by others during sparring. My saving grace was that I tossed a black belt over my shoulder like a sack of potatoes and easily broke my first board with a solid, powerful back kick. Still, I walked out of the school frustrated, disappointed, and embarrassed.

That night I turned to my prayer table, where I asked the Universe for guidance, comfort, and help to accept my imperfections. So far, praying had done wonders for me. But when I forgot to pray, perfectionism reared its ugly head; it ruined my serenity and tore down my confidence.

So, I prayed that night for guidance.

The Universe said nothing.

Or so I thought.

I ultimately gave up and went to bed. I didn't think anyone or anything heard me.

IN the months that followed, I blossomed. Green belt represented a tremendous time of growth—mentally, physically, and spiritually. I felt like a tree that had finally taken root and sprouted newborn twigs. My forms and stances were more solid than ever. I was getting closer to the floor in a 170-degree split. All those kicks I had practiced were now whipping my uniform like a popping towel. When Kyoshi pulled out four-foot candleholders and instructed me to extinguish the burning flame with a fast, snapping kick or punch, I did so without ever hitting the flame or knocking over the candle.

Life was improving spiritually as well. Once a week, I met with two Catholic women from my sober meetings to meditate. On Sundays I joined Kyoshi and Terri for Daystar Church services. I'd been sober for eighteen months, and I felt good; the pieces to life's puzzle were finally fitting into place.

BUOYED by newfound confidence, I passed another belt exam, breaking my first cement block with a knife-hand strike. By summer, I was a bright blue belt, learning the *bo* form that I watched Kyoshi perform not so long ago. I loved learning my first weapon, but I was a hopeless klutz and regularly whacked my elbow and head with the wooden *bo*'s ends.

Martial arts was helping me find balance in my life. I even

started spending more time with Mamma, who was now remarried. She teetered between pressuring me to find a job—any job—and questioning me about why I spent so much time training. She didn't understand why I was drawn to martial arts, or why I needed or wanted to learn to use three different parts of my foot to break boards, thwart an attack with a hip throw, or finally break the wrist hold of someone stronger than Ed.

Unemployment had been a gift for several months, and I'd had a blast spending every day pretending that I was a Shaolin Temple monk. Reality set in, though, and I began looking for another job. I doubted I'd be able to stay in San Antonio if I wanted to work in newspapers again.

33

AT a sober meeting one day, I heard that "coincidences are God's way of performing miracles anonymously." I didn't know if I believed that, but my facts-based mind had to acknowledge that right when I needed reassurance, I'd see a fish decal.

Slowly, my heart opened to a spiritual realm. Serendipity was now common, and I was starting to feel less shocked and more accepting that there was a Higher Power in the Universe.

I was still learning about Jesus and the Bible, but I was more drawn to Buddhism than Christianity. Grasshopper was Buddhist. It felt natural. Simple. Peaceful.

Still, I tried to keep an open mind.

DURING the self-defense portion of another belt exam, Kyoshi sat in his black swivel chair on the hardwood floor. This rank required me to show forty-five techniques.

"How many do you know?" Kyoshi asked.

"Thirty-three," I answered immediately. I knew it wasn't enough, but it's what suddenly rolled out of my mouth. Maybe it was because earlier in the day I'd learned that Jesus died at age 33.

"Thirty-three," Kyoshi said. "That's a very specific number."

I shrugged my shoulders. He ordered me to begin.

The demonstration began purposeful and methodical. I knew exactly what technique to do and what technique was next, and I felt confident that Kyoshi was writing down positive notes on my exam sheet. At some point, though, I forgot the order of some techniques, and what number I was on, so I just began showing any technique I could remember.

Suddenly, I came to a stopping point.

"That's all I know, sir," I said.

"That's all?" Kyoshi asked, raising a single eyebrow.

"Yes, sir," I said. Already drenched in sweat, I had begun to mentally sweat.

"Wow," Kyoshi said, looking down at my exam sheet.

I began to fear I'd failed.

"Do you know how many techniques you did?" he asked.

"No, sir," I said. "I lost track."

"You did exactly 33," he said, nodding in approval.

I passed.

Coincidence?

I tried not to analyze it, yet I never forgot that day.

If You're Going Through Hell, Keep Going

DREAM: I'm on a merry-go-round, and there is circus music play-
ing. The songs are lively; the mood is joyful. Then the music changes
tone and the merry-go-round is no longer fun. I am in despair, and
I don't know how to stop going round and round. Clowns are
nearby. They're running away from the circus. They urge me to
jump onto the miniature train they have waiting. I jump on the train,
and we ride from the circus grounds into a lush field of grass and
wheat. Eventually, we all get out of the train and go our separate
ways.

SEVEN months of unemployment and a rapidly dwindling bank account later, I accepted a job offer from the *Austin American-States-*
man, seventy-five miles up Interstate 35 in the state's hip capital
city. The newspaper wanted me, but I wasn't sure I wanted it, especially now that I had settled down somewhere, now that I had
friends, and now that I had Kyoshi. I had a real life now, and I didn't
want to leave San Antonio. Yet the geographic fix was in—this time
without any of my doing—and if I wanted to work again, I'd have
to pack up and move to Austin.

For months after moving to Austin, I commuted to San Antonio
to train with Kyoshi twice a week on my days off from the newspaper. During the week in Austin, I studied kuk sool won karate.
Learning two different styles of martial arts at the same time was
exhilarating until it became confusing, and soon the one hundred-
fifty-mile round-trip drive to San Antonio became time-consum-
ing—and spiritually confusing.

More and more, Kyoshi openly preached about Jesus and the Bible. And while talking about current affairs, he voiced negative views on homosexuals.

This worried me, as I was coming to terms with being gay.

All these years later, I was finally able to tell someone that my college fling was with another woman. I was so ashamed of myself, and I didn't want anyone but Hilda to know.

I suspected Kyoshi already knew, but I tried to hide it. I felt confused, hurt, and ashamed. And I feared Kyoshi would hate me if I ever told him. But every time I pretended I could be straight, I felt anxious and wanted to drink. Thus far, acceptance of who I truly was had kept me sober.

Slowly, the love and admiration I felt for Kyoshi waned as I battled shame every time we trained. Our relationship had become a muddied mixture of teacher-student, friend-mentor, "Are you coming to Daystar Church this Sunday?" confusion. He was slipping from the pedestal I'd placed him on for years, and though I still craved his approval, I no longer saw him as the father figure I'd always wanted. I wasn't just going through physical trials with Kyoshi anymore. My greatest life lessons now involved spiritual turmoil.

I yearned for a return to the early training days when I was comforted by the small sign hanging above Kyoshi's ballet barre that read: "He is the way, the truth, and the light." Knowing that Kyoshi and Jesus were good friends made me feel safe and warm. Now, though, I was torn between my buffet-style spiritual beliefs and Kyoshi's Bible-based interpretation of God. I began to wonder what the hell religion had to do with getting a black belt.

THROUGH lots of work in therapy and meditation with my Catholic peeps, I was trying to accept being gay. And if I hadn't been overcome with shame, Kyoshi's abhorrence for homosexuality may not have had power.

But I was vulnerable, weak, and scared.

Maybe God will strike me down for being gay, I thought.

"Cathy, you know that's not true," Hilda said. "God loves you. He made you just the way you are for a reason. Did you turn your will and your life over to God when you got sober?"

"Yes," I said in tears.

"And are you still gay?"

"Yes."

"Then don't argue with Him."

Despite Hilda's comforting words, like a child who wants the love of her father, I still wanted Kyoshi's approval. To be fair, he never asked for this admiration. I put him on a pedestal. And I'd have to take him off. So I kept asking questions, trying to find a way to tell him the truth.

One day I sucked it up.

"If you had to sum up Jesus's message in the Bible in one sentence," I asked Kyoshi in his office, "what would you say was his message?"

It was a trick question; I knew what he'd say.

"Love."

I reared back to throw a verbal left hook. "So what's so bad about love?"

"Nothing."

"So what's so bad about two women or two men loving each other?"

"You mean like in California where the boys wanna marry the boys?" he laughed, and then more seriously said, "It's unnatural."

"Love's unnatural?"

"No. The act is unnatural. God honors the union of a man and a woman."

"But love is Jesus's message, right? That's what you just said."

"Not *that* kind of love," he said, his eyebrows evening out.

"Well, then I don't understand. What's right love?"

For the next ten minutes, Kyoshi gave a long-winded sermon, tossing out scripture quotes as fast and furious as a batting cage machine propels baseballs. Passionate and authoritative, he picked up momentum with every verse he cited. Listening to him, I sank into my chair, filled with shame and confusion. His stern stance crushed my spirit. I loved him so much, and yet he was so obviously disgusted with me and who I really was.

Despite feeling hurt, embarrassed, and ashamed, I came clean.

"Well, you may have already figured this out already, but I'm gay."

Kyoshi sat back in his chair, quiet for a while. Then he began a whirlwind citation of more scripture verses, after which he issued a challenge:

Read the Bible.

"If you find anything that justifies that lifestyle, I'd like to see it. I want to know."

"O.K., I will," I promised, my voice quivering. I wasn't sure I'd read it. But I had to say something so I could leave his office. I was about to burst into tears, and I didn't want him to see me cry. I tried my best to keep my emotions in check as I left. Pulling out of the parking lot, I began to sob hard—snot dripping on my seat belt strap—all the way back to Austin.

Later that night, Hilda provided her usual, gentle perspective. I was so hurt that Kyoshi couldn't accept me for who I was. She reminded me that many spiritual texts guide people in the world and that the Bible was just one of them.

"We alcoholics have our own book, and that text says that 'we ceased fighting everything and everyone,'" Hilda said.

She was annoying, pointing out that I had no control over whether Kyoshi accepted me as I was, only over whether I accepted him as *he* was.

"But how can I face him?" I charged back. "I've already prayed and meditated long enough to know this is me."

"The only person you have to answer to is your Higher Power. If anyone wants you to justify your life, tell them to make an appointment with God and let them hash it out."

She was right again.

Through more writing, therapy, prayer, and meditation, I slowly was able to see my part in it all: I'd started this whole mess by overstepping the boundaries of my teacher-student relationship with Kyoshi by going to his church, and I had no place to question him on his beliefs. He was my karate instructor, not my father; a man, not a god. If Kyoshi thought that I was going to hell, I'd have to accept that. It was what he believed. It wasn't my job to challenge or change him.

How I would get a black belt from him, though, was another story.

"More will be revealed," Hilda said in her usual soft, peaceful voice. "Get down on your knees and ask your Higher Power for clarity. Keep it simple until then."

Keep It Simple

MASTER Po told Student Caine, "Never forget that a priest's life is a simple one."

Before moving to Austin, I donated my couch, desk, bed, and a closet full of clothes to the neighborhood thrift store.

Save a simple meditation table, the living room of my Austin apartment was bare: No furniture, wall decorations, or clutter. It was calm and quiet, lacking that crazy, lived-in feeling. When I moved in, I stood in the doorway, looking at the drab brown carpet and partial brick walls, vowing to never bring anything into the space that wouldn't contribute to peace.

Like Grasshopper in the Shaolin Temple, I lived humbly in that one-bedroom apartment a block from the newspaper, I slept on the floor atop a twin-sized air mattress, ate meals sitting on the bare carpeted floor, and continued nightly meditation at my prayer table.

Despite extreme efforts to keep my home clean and serene, I continued to battle a low-grade depression. But I was still sober, and I continued to seek the source of serenity and happiness.

I was convinced that I'd find it through martial arts.

Good-bye

LIFE resembled the months following the Thanksgiving Day fiasco. Though I continued to train with Kyoshi, my heart wasn't in it.

I battled insecurity, even though I'd recently broken my first cement block with the blade of my hand. That break was easy compared to Kyoshi's current spiritual expectations.

As recommended in my sober program, I suited up and showed up. Every time I wanted to quit, my eyes met that damn Don't Quit sign. Maybe it was all in my mind, but I sensed that more and more I fell short of Kyoshi's expectations, especially regarding my spiritual progress. The nervous admiration I felt for him in the beginning, when I used to watch him train before class in God-like awe, was replaced by an awkward apprehension. Even though I had almost two years of sobriety, I thought about drinking again.

Now that he knew I was gay, would he hold it against me? Would he withhold a black belt if I didn't accept Jesus Christ as my lord and savior?

I was confused and hurt, so I took some time off from studying with Kyoshi, training full time in Austin and jogging around Lady Bird Lake to improve my sloth-like quickness and long-distance endurance. When I finally returned to San Antonio, Kyoshi greeted me warmly at the front door. As soon as I saw his face, though, I knew he was dying to know what, if anything, I'd learned from reading the Bible.

"Did you get the chance to do that reading we talked about?" he asked one day, almost pleadingly.

"No, I didn't," I said. I had to be honest.

It was the first time I'd refused to follow his instructions.

Kyoshi looked at me with different eyes—partly sad, mostly disappointed—and dropped the subject. I knew we'd never again discuss the Bible, Jesus, or gays again.

I knew I had to leave Kyoshi. After my last class, as I started to walk out the door, a knot grew in my throat. I looked into Kyoshi's eyes. For more than two years, he'd been the solid, strong, demanding, and guiding-force father figure I'd always wanted and needed. Despite the pain of not being accepted, I loved him deeply and knew that I would miss him terribly. That night, for the first time, I saw in his eyes that he would miss me, too.

In the end, we silently agreed to disagree on whether gays were destined for hell, and he wished me well in my training in Austin.

"I love you," he said, giving me a warm hug with his strong, Popeye-like arms. "God bless you. Come back anytime."

"I will, sir," I said, feeling heartbroken. I knew it would be a long time before I could come back.

Again, I cried all the way back to Austin. But despite the tears, I was still willing to try this martial arts thing again.

I left a red belt, the seventh in a nine-belt system. Now instead of chasing a yellow belt, I was after a black belt. What I still longed for, though, was the comfort, serenity, and simplicity of Grasshopper, and that night I had a prophetic dream:

I'm walking alone along an endless highway on a hot day with a backpack strapped to my shoulders. My hair is long and stringy, and I have a bandana tied around my forehead. I'm bored, tapping a green road sign as I pass. I don't worry about how far the next town is. I know now that I'll make it. I'm not tired. I'm not afraid anymore. I know I'll make it.

Searching for Grasshopper

Cathy Chapaty

Part III

The Dojo Shuffle

Cathy Chapaty

Just Keep Moving

MY new martial arts instructor was a fantastic technician with an energizing presence. Charming, charismatic, and handsome, he was instantly likable. In a small carpeted studio in a strip mall, I sat on the school's benches and watched in awe as the instructor practiced new jiu-jitsu grappling techniques he'd learned while training with Brazil's famed Gracie family. I was impressed, grateful to have a new master and a new home. Plus it didn't hurt that I thought the black uniform I now wore made me look a little thinner.

At the new school, I began the road to black belt all over again as a lowly white belt.

KUK sool won forms seemed boring compared to Kyoshi's eclectic patterns, and the instructor's cardiovascular workout wasn't as intense, but the self-defense techniques were fun to learn. I attended noon classes regularly, studied hard, and in a few months qualified for a yellow belt.

While attaining yellow at Kyoshi's school catapulted my confidence, a yellow belt in kuk sool won raised neither my heart rate nor passion. I couldn't stop comparing my new instructor to Kyoshi. The new guy was a solid martial artist, but he rarely led class. The day-to-day instruction was often led by his black belts. Kyoshi always led class. I expected the same treatment. Maybe I'd been spoiled, for I learned that not every student was lucky enough to receive instruction from the source.

Discouraged and out hundreds of dollars in contract fees, I had to admit that kuk sool won wasn't for me and that this instructor also wasn't the Master Po of my Grasshopper dreams.

It wasn't his fault.

It wasn't my fault, either.

I moved on.

ONE night while heading to a sandwich shop across the street from the newspaper offices, I noticed a dojo in a simple, warehouse-like building. Eventually, curiosity won, and I strolled over to watch a class at the all-female Sun Dragon Martial Arts.

Well, this is different, I thought.

Women of all shapes and sizes sporting long hair, short hair, purple hair, and buzz cuts stood in perfect lines doing kicking drills as the instructor counted in Japanese. One big woman, in particular, caught my eye. She sported a flat-top haircut, large breasts, and wore a tank top that revealed tattoos all over her upper body. I was immediately afraid. These women had powerful spirits.

The dojo resembled a dark cave. Plastic-wrapped windows kept out what little sunshine was left at 6 p.m. The floors were carpeted here, too, and I began to think that Kyoshi had the only wooden dojo floor in Texas.

The instructor approached me at the break. Sensei Suzanne was pleasant, confident, and authoritative. But what sold me on Sun Dragon was that there were no contracts. After my last experience, I didn't want to be tied down to an expensive, long-term commitment.

"Fifty dollars a month," Sensei said. "But if you can't pay that, I'll work with you."

"Sounds good to me," I said.

And just like that, I started my road to black belt all over again as a lowly white belt.

AT Sun Dragon, Sensei taught the Japanese style of kyokushin karate. Like Kyoshi, Sensei was the owner and sole instructor of the school. She lived at Sun Dragon—literally—in a small, oblong office/living room/bedroom area just off the dojo floor. I admired the humble simplicity.

Although Sensei counted in Japanese during basic training drills and practiced traditional forms, Sun Dragon was anything but a traditional dojo. Fleetwood Mac often blared on the stereo during sparring class because Sensei thought students sparred better to music. After Tuesday night classes, some women stayed for meditation, forming a silent circle around a single candle as the sun disappeared at dusk. After meditation, some of the remaining women flocked to the nearby and frigid Barton Springs for a cold dip. I never joined them, trying to maintain firm boundaries with instructors and classmates.

Sun Dragon's greatest strength was its community—a strong social circle in which everyone pulled together to help each other. One spring, the school held a garage sale to fund scholarships for women who otherwise couldn't afford to go to a women's martial arts camp. Sensei was a great motivator and supporter of this particular training opportunity, and every woman who wanted to attend the National Women's Martial Arts Federation camp at Texas Woman's University in Denton did. Even me.

The camp was an eye-opener. I'd never seen so many women train together before. I'd never seen so many women black belts either. And I was stunned by the variety of martial arts styles represented, many of which I'd never heard of before.

Sun Dragon was a good school; my classmates were fun, encouraging, and supportive, and it was nice to bond with other women who had a common desire and love for martial arts. There were other lesbians on the mat. I no longer felt so alone. And it was safe and comforting to no longer be the only woman amid a sea of male students.

I always wondered where all the other women trained.

Now I knew.

They were at Sun Dragon.

Despite the school's welcoming atmosphere, though, a familiar restlessness and uneasiness returned.

Six months later, the novelty of all-female training wore off. I actually missed working out with men. I needed men. If I could toss a man over my shoulder or floor him with a swift judo sweep, I had fewer doubts about defending myself in a real attack.

A void remained. Eventually, I accepted that kyokushin and the women of Sun Dragon still weren't the path to peace I sought.

I didn't say good-bye to anyone.

I just moved on.

MONTHS passed. Pounds amassed on my couch-potato body. The first signs of a previously dormant depression reappeared. Praying was not enough. It was time to take action. I was on a renewed mission.

With Austin yellow pages in hand, I decided to visit as many martial arts schools as I could find. I took advantage of every free workout and trial special, and observed hours of classes in American kenpo, karate, aikido, and more taekwondo. I studied the instructors—how they talked to their students, what they deemed appropriate discipline, and whether they instilled fear or bred self-confidence. I spoke with one master after another, quizzing them about their philosophy and background, finding out who provided the instruction.

I was appalled and discouraged at the less-than-stellar quality of some schools. There were womanizing instructors, beer-belly black belts, and the worst sin of all, arrogant asses. I wasn't impressed and became even more disillusioned.

Cognitively I knew *Kung Fu* was just a TV show, but was an honorable, courageous, humble, and selfless way of life through martial arts training so unattainable in modern-day America? It was heartbreaking to think that maybe my idea of the ideal way of life was an illusion, that maybe martial arts wasn't the path to peace after all. I loved martial arts, yet thought about quitting forever.

Then I remembered Kyoshi's damn Don't Quit sign, and I realized that I couldn't stop now. I had to trudge on.

My Instructor Is Trying to Kill Me

AS I wandered around a north Austin mini-mall on a hot August afternoon, I saw an interesting-looking taekwondo school tucked between a hobby shop and a Chinese restaurant. I recalled seeing the school's ad in the yellow pages touting "Olympic-Style Taekwondo Training." I went in.

The school was smaller than the outside let on. Stray shoes sat in slots on a wooden shelf. A Republic of South Korea flag hung prominently above a wall of mirrors. As I scanned the room, I was mesmerized by all the unevenly hung, framed photographs of the master instructor breaking stacks of bricks and boards with an assortment of body parts.

The school was empty. I felt awkward standing there alone, as if I was trespassing on sacred ground. My gut was telling me to leave, yet I remained. Finally, an extremely thin Asian man with short, spiky hair appeared from a back room. He wore an old, worn V-neck taekwondo uniform and had an even more tattered, seven-striped black belt around his waist. The edges were so frayed that the belt took on a grayish hue. Speaking poor English, he invited me into his school.

"Please remove shoes?" he said, bowing as he shook my hand.

"Oh, yes sir!" I said, quickly pulling off my new white Reeboks and putting them in one of the wooden shoe-shelf slots.

His accent was so thick that I barely understood him. But Master C did manage to communicate the school's two-month summer special—three months if I had my own uniform. And in a matter of minutes, the search for peace and happiness was alive again as I

73

signed the standard paperwork and wrote a check. Convinced that I had finally found the ideal Asian instructor I'd always dreamed of (at the time, I erroneously believed I'd have a more authentic martial arts experience training with an Asian) and relieved that I'd finally found a new home, I poured all my energy into the school and my new instructor.

I started the road to black belt all over again as a lowly white belt.

MASTER C taught his own classes, and he was strict. He had a fondness for discipline through push-ups. If students were late to class, they had to pump out at least thirty push-ups—depending on how late they were—and kneel at the edge of the mat until Master C acknowledged and invited them to class. Sometimes he purposefully ignored them.

"American lazy people," he complained. "Ver lazy. No wan work hard."

My first day ended up being an endurance workout from hell. I was the only white belt there; the other students were intermediate green and advanced blue belts. Master C seemed a little perturbed because two students arrived late. He decided we needed discipline. We worked on kicks. And more kicks. And more advanced kicks. Then spinning kicks. And jumping kicks.

"Was amatah you?" he uttered to me in his broken English. "You lazy American no eah yo Wheaties today?"

I frowned, wondering why he was picking on me.

"You all lazy," he said, throwing his hands down in disgust after bowing and dismissing the class. I stood there at the edge of the mat, facing the South Korean flag, wondering what just happened. Everyone else bowed off the mat, grabbed their gym bags, and said their good-byes to one another as if the day's treatment was normal. Maybe it was. Maybe I was the one who wasn't normal. Maybe I really was lazy.

Great. I thought. *Now I'm crazy AND lazy.*

The next day, I was the sorest I'd been since my early days with Kyoshi. This made me strangely happy. I vowed that Master C would never accuse me of being lazy again.

Unlike kuk sool won and kyokushin, taekwondo was very quickly rekindling the fighting spirit in me. I felt like I was back in Master Pliska's class again and I loved everything about the training. The kicks, punches, and forms were solid and powerful, and I felt invigorated. My Asian master was tough and a perfectionist like Kyoshi, but surprisingly and suddenly encouraging of me in particular. It was obvious that he liked me, and that made me instantly want him to like me even more. Unlike with Kyoshi, my desire to do my best for Master C wasn't prompted by a feeling of admiration and respect. This man scared the dickens out of me. I worked hard for him because of two things: I didn't want to be labeled a "lazy American" and I didn't want to die at his hands. I blew off the fact that sometimes I picked up a weird vibe or two and was sometimes uncomfortable around him. I couldn't figure it out so I ignored it.

Again, I was regularly the only female in a noon class full of big, strong men. But the Monday of my third week of training, I was the only *student* in the class. I couldn't tell if Master C was mad at his missing students or at me, but without warning, he put me through a martial arts physical pop quiz, ordering me to perform the kicking and punching drills I'd been learning. Next, I demonstrated the white belt form. Later, we sparred. Lastly, push-ups. Ten, t-w-e-n-t-y, t..h..i..r..t..y. I was waiting for him to tell me to stop, but he never did.

"You no stop!" he shouted in my ear as he got down on all fours and in my face. "You lazy American? You go! You keep go!"

My arms were weak, wobbly, and slowly failing me. Suddenly, I felt a jerk from above. Master C reached down and grabbed my uniform collar from the back of the neck. He yanked me up in the air then smashed my face down to the floor—up and down, up and down—until I finished the push-up drill.

I swore he was trying to kill me.

He thought I was ready for a promotion.

"You ready foh yellow," he declared.

"Really?" I said between breaths. "Thank you, sir."

"Ya. Wednesday."

"O.K., sir. Thank you, sir," I said, bowing with a proud grin.

Yellow belt—and so quickly, too.

I felt a baffling combination of happiness and uneasiness. I wanted to move up the ranks as soon as possible now that I had rekindled my passion, but I expected it would take at least three months for me to qualify for a promotion in a new art. After all, I had only been training at the school less than a month. Yet there Master C stood—authoritative despite his broken English—offering me a yellow belt. I was flattered, and I was afraid of being disrespectful if I refused. I'd already made that mistake with Master Pliska, and I figured the best way to make amends for running away from him then was to change my behavior going forward.

Two days later, I drove to the mall as usual, parking my car and uttering my standard before-training prayer:

God, please do for me what I cannot do for myself and please protect me from injury and harm with complete abandon.

As I walked up to the school, I noticed a handwritten note taped to the outside of the door.

Close due family emergincy.

The doors were locked. I stood at the school's entrance for a while, at first worried about the welfare of Master C and his family, then disappointed that I wouldn't get to test for a yellow belt.

I didn't want to let a perfectly good training day go to waste, so I strolled over to a martial arts supply store and training facility around the corner in the same mall. I paid the user fee, whaled on the punching bag, hit the heavy bag with some hard kicks, and practiced forms.

After about an hour, I headed out, stopping at the front counter to chat with the owner about the note on Master C's door.

"Do you know what happened?" I asked.

The owner laughed hard, shaking his head in judgment.

"Is *that* what it says? Some emergency," he lured. "You mean you don't know why he's not there today?"

"No," I said, shrugging, "I just saw the note."

"I see," he said, leaning forward and whispering, "Well, it's because one of his female black belt students accused him of sexual assault. He's in jail."

My jaw dropped.

"If I were you," he continued, "I'd find somewhere else to train."

I stood at the counter, mouth agape, unable to move, paralyzed by the news. I swallowed hard and aimlessly walked out the door. On the way to my car, I thought about Monday's class when I was alone with him, the only female, the *only* student. I knew something was nagging me about him and his manner. I was about to get really angry with myself for being so naive and gullible—for not trusting my instincts. Then I remembered that I had said my standard prayer that Monday, too:

God, please do for me what I cannot do for myself, and please protect me from injury and harm with complete abandon.

My prayer had amazingly been answered exactly the way I said it. As I took one last look at the school, I sighed in relief, whispered a spiritual thanks to the Universe, and drove home.

The next morning, a short *Austin American-Statesman* article detailed the alleged assault and my instructor's arrest.

The school closed immediately afterward, and he dropped off the radar. I didn't know whether Master C was ever convicted, cleared, or acquitted of the charge. I never saw him again, and although I was out $100 in tuition, I was unharmed.

Not such a bad deal—or lesson—after all.

Again, I was frustratingly back at square one. This time I had no choice: I had to move on.

Full Circle

IN time, the shock, relief, and disappointment of the Master C experience faded. In its place was another phase of feeling disillusioned by the martial arts way of life.

I took a break from searching for the perfect dojo, and when I finally felt ready to try again, I rewrote my Shaolin Temple "must-haves" list:

1. *A black belt is no longer important.*
2. *I don't care anymore whether the school has hardwood floors or carpet.*
3. *It doesn't matter whether I train with men or women.*
4. *I don't care if students spar to music or drumming.*
5. *If sweat is involved, I'll take it.*

I just wanted to train again. I just wanted a little peace and somewhere to sit down and stay awhile. Surely there was a place out there for me, but since leaving Kyoshi, I'd been unable to settle down and grow. I'd already spent a lot of money and years trying to find peace. I doubted I'd ever be happy training anywhere again.

Hilda always said to pray for clarity, so I did. I hoped that the adage "when the student is ready, the teacher will appear" was true. I thought I was ready again, so I resumed my search.

On an overcast, drizzly, and dreary October afternoon, I drove down a slick street, passing the University of Texas campus. I recalled the taekwondo class I took during my last semester at the university—and Master Pliska. After all these years, I still remembered his name, and still regretted running from his invitation to test.

Where might I be today had I just taken that yellow belt test?

A loose stack of crumpled yellow pages was strewn all over the passenger seat. I glanced at the last page as I waited for a green light. I was down to the U's in the yellow pages and on the verge of heartbreak. I still hadn't found my idyllic Shaolin Temple in Texas.

Next up and last listed: United States Martial Arts Institute. It was farther down the road at the corner of Guadalupe and 43rd, but it seemed so far away. I felt discouraged, exhausted, and sad. All I wanted was a home again. I needed this place to be the one.

Pulling into the parking lot, I got my first glance at the facility: another old warehouse-like building. It was painted an ominous gray and sported old garage doors. It was the drabbest place I'd ever seen. As I sat buckled up in my car, I shook my head, then took a few deep breaths and said a prayer:

God, I'm so tired. I don't know if I should even do this martial arts stuff anymore. Nothing seems to be going right. Is it over for me? Do I need to let this go? I'm going in, but this is it. If this isn't the place for me, I'm not looking anymore. I'm just going to accept that my time in the martial arts is over, Grasshopper was just a dream, and that I was never meant to find peace through martial arts.

The light drizzle outside turned into a hard rain, but I got out of my car anyway and trotted through the puddle-filled parking lot and into the school's entrance. Once in the doorway, I bowed and was struck by an overpowering stench of sweat. The lights were out, but I could see a huge, cream-colored judo mat covering the floor. The U.S. and South Korean flags hung above a wall-to-wall mirror at the front, and two long punching bags hung from metal rafters. There was a sea of plaques, trophies, and awards on top of a glass case that held an assortment of uniforms, sparring gear, and belts. The place reeked so badly of perspiration that I smiled; I only found that scent in schools where the students trained hard. The bloodstain on the edge of the mat oddly didn't scare me.

As I reached a hand to knock on the door of the office, the door suddenly flew open and a tall, lanky fellow in street clothes emerged. He had light brown curly hair, a mole on his cheek—and looked awfully familiar.

"Hi! What can I do for you?" the man said, smiling.

"I'm interested in knowing a little bit about your school."

"O.K. Have you trained before?"

"Yes, sir. I took taekwondo in college, and I studied an eclectic style of karate with an instructor in San Antonio."

"You take taekwondo at UT?"

"Yes, sir," I said, studying his face. He looked *so* familiar.

Then it hit me:

Tall and lanky.

Mole on his cheek.

Curly hair.

I looked hard at his face, and a chill shimmied down my spine.

"Master Pliska?" I asked.

"Yeah, James Pliska," he said, reaching out his large palm for a handshake. "I thought I knew you."

"Oh, wow, sir," I said like a giddy groupie finally meeting her rock music idol. "I can't believe this."

We chatted for a few minutes, giving *Cliff Notes* versions of where we each had been since my time at UT, and he invited me to return that evening to watch a class. I gratefully accepted.

In the driver's seat of my car, I strapped on the seat belt, put both hands on the steering wheel, and stared out the windshield—stunned, grateful, and teary-eyed. After all the searching, I had come full circle, and it was clear that the Universe was giving me a second chance to finish what I started.

I had a feeling that I'd be here awhile.

Searching for Grasshopper

Cathy Chapaty

Part IV

Black Belt or Bust

Cathy Chapaty

Button-Pushin' Black Belts

WHAT goes around comes around.

As soon as I got into a long-desired groove of training with Master Pliska, he left Austin for a job in Alamo, Texas—ditched me as fast as I had ditched him and that yellow belt test in the fall of 1986.

The school's founder and grandmaster, Dr. Daeshik Kim, limited his teaching to the University of Texas taekwondo and judo programs. So Master Pliska left the school in the hands of a large and capable army of black belts, led by Master Mike, a small yet tremendously powerful and energetic, old-school taekwondo teacher. This guy kicked and punched harder than anyone I'd ever met. Harder than Kyoshi. As the newest student, I stood in the back row, watching and hearing his uniform snap and pop with every move. I was so mesmerized that at times I forgot to do the punches and kicks myself.

"Join us anytime, Cathy," Master Mike said.

"Yes, sir!" I'd reply.

Master Mike awed and intimidated me. I didn't look up to him like I did Kyoshi—not because Master Mike was about my height and there was no need to look up, but rather because he told me the truth, just like Hilda. I didn't like the truth because it often hurt my little feelings. But I had to admit that so far, he was always right.

Master Mike was a fan of commitment and consistency, and he told me early on that I didn't have either. I was a lowly white belt again, with no responsibility to others or expectations of myself. It showed. I wanted to work out, but I didn't want there to be *too* much work involved.

Like a stubborn child throwing a temper tantrum, I mumbled my complaints under my breath, detesting the manner in which everyone trained. Didn't these people know that they weren't doing things like Kyoshi? Didn't they know that the cushy, heavy denim judo mat made it impossible to hold a good, solid horse stance? I never had problems holding a horse stance on Kyoshi's wooden floors, yet now my feet slowly slid apart during every warm-up. Didn't they know that real dojos had real wooden floors?

My instructors and fellow classmates didn't seem to mind the school's obvious physical defects, ignoring the fact that the old building had nothing but ceiling fans and garage doors for air conditioning and toilets that flushed only when the handle was held down on Tuesday evenings during a full moon. Everyone simply focused on their training.

Nitpicky black belts corrected every detail of my blocks, kicks, and punches, pushing already-raw insecurity buttons down to the nerve. Each class provided new opportunities to suck air from rounds of lap running, never-ending jumping jacks, judo push-ups, and high-speed, endurance-building kicking drills. Kyoshi may have pushed me to my spiritual limit, but these instructors pushed my physical threshold. Irrational resentment grew, spurred by the prideful realization that I couldn't maintain the black belts' pace.

I took a few months off from training.

I couldn't be the problem, I defiantly thought.

Two months later: *Maybe it is me.*

When I got past the minor irritations—the uncomfortable heat and humidity, annoying toilets, and demanding pace—my biggest gripe was that despite years of martial arts training, I was being treated as if I were the lowly white belt I wore again. Instructors never gave me credit for what I already knew. As if they sensed that I was struggling with arrogance, the black belts seemed hell-bent on exorcising the ego demon from my soul by pure, hard, sweat-drenching, no-bells-and-whistles, in-your-face training.

I didn't like how I was being treated, and at first, my ego contributed to a lack of regular attendance. The times I did manage to put my pride aside and attend class, I felt as if I had two left feet. By the end of every class, my legs were as heavy as cement, and my arms were fleshy, odor-reeking rubber bands. Although I was more than ready to bolt to another school, I did a rare thing: I stayed. After all, having visited almost every other school in town, I knew there was nowhere else to go.

Months of irritability, restlessness, and discontentment followed until I got it through my thick skull to humble myself and ask for guidance.

"You're inconsistent," Master Mike quipped during a one-on-one conference in Dr. Kim's office. Holding a No. 2 pencil in one hand, he leaned back and swiveled around in an old chair that was in dire need of WD-40. Clean-cut and clean-shaven except for a hairy chest, Master Mike wore his trademark tattered black belt with white, frayed edges and five gold stripes around a well-used and dingy white V-neck uniform.

"You just need to come to class more often and you'll get the hang of it around here," he said.

Master Mike proposed that I set a goal to be evaluated during the next rank exam as a blue belt.

"Blue?" I said, flattered.

"Cathy, everybody knows you're no white belt. But you're acting like one. You need to be more consistent in your training. You need to show up more."

"Yes, sir," I said to him.

I hate you, I said to myself. *How dare you question my commitment to martial arts? What an ass!*

I walked out of the office with that familiar sting in my nose, the quiver of my bottom lip, and the immediate need to get out to my car before anyone saw me cry. His words hurt, mostly because when I quit whining, I knew he was right. My meditation book confirmed it. The next day's entry read: "We may fight change, even a small one, because our ego is invested in how it *was*."

I missed Kyoshi.

My attitude didn't change overnight, but I went to sleep every evening and awoke every morning with Master Mike's words ringing in my ears. Why was I rebelling? Why was I resisting the invitation to walk a new path? Starting over, unlearning everything Kyoshi taught me, and opening myself to a new way felt like an ugly and selfish betrayal of my beloved teacher. I didn't want to let go of what Kyoshi taught me. I didn't want to lose the growth and confidence he instilled in me. I just couldn't bear to let go. So I didn't, and for a while longer I remained stuck.

Austin martial arts legend Brian Duffy proved to be a wise mentor placed in my path at the right time. During my rebellion phase, he gave me a private trial class. I liked the workout, and I asked to join his school. Knowing my past, he politely refused.

"I think you need to go back to that school and finish what you started first," he said.

I knew he was right.

Still, I remained stubborn. And six months of consistent, inconsistent training later, I remained a white belt. Had it not been for my best buddy, Susan, I might still be a white belt today.

Susan, a short-haired, thin ball of energy wrapped in a Maine accent, signed up for the school's two-month trial program and insisted that I show her the ropes. I obliged and recommitted myself to regular attendance. Two training sessions later, Susan quit, but soon afterward, I had an odd, prophetic-like dream that helped me turn an important corner:

I'm in a high school gym with other students practicing karate. An old, short Asian man with gray hair and an aging black belt approaches me. "Why are you standing there?" he asks. "Time for you to train. You need to train hard. We been waiting for you. Get busy!"

Called by a higher source, I answered. One class at a time, my attendance—and not surprisingly my attitude and technique—improved.

"You've got a great front kick," said Okkie, a slender, early 20s black belt. "It's not as good as mine, but it's not bad."

Never comfortable with taking a compliment, I immediately suspected Okkie wanted something from me. I expected him to invite me out for dinner and drinks after class. He didn't. Okkie just stood there, arms folded just above his gold-striped black belt, curiously watching me and occasionally laughing when I lost my balance during kicking drills.

For some reason, he liked me.

I decided I liked him, too.

Friendships with other students blossomed, and soon classmates started pestering me about when I would trade in my now-dirty white belt for a yellow one. But since I was having a good time again—simply training, sweating, stretching, and kicking—I didn't want to jinx anything. I was finally comfortable in my new home. As a lowly white belt, I felt no pressure from stressful exams. I felt no expectations and had no responsibilities. I reveled in being nothing. Through more sober step work, though, the truth emerged: My white belt had become another Kyoshi, another thing I didn't want to release.

Classmates became more prodding and persistent. It was as if they called one another before class and rehearsed the same question: "When are you going to test?"

Even the assistant instructors chimed in.

"You still have that white belt?" asked "Big Ron" Hutto, a firefighter and fourth-degree black belt with an endearing, thick Texas drawl. A towering teddy bear built of a lean wall of muscle and topped by a tight crew cut, Ron was surprisingly gentle and had an encouraging nature. I admired how he gave everything he had every time he trained. Ron never failed to leave behind a big puddle of sweat on the mat after class was over. I liked him a lot. I wanted to be like him. I wanted to one day leave sweat puddles in my wake, too.

Ron shook his head, scratched his Texas National Guard crew-cut scalp, and said, "I thought fur sure you'd be green b'now."

"I know, sir," I said softly, looking down.

"Whatcha waitin' fur? Permission? Hell, I'll give you my O.K. You're ready."

"Yes, sir," I said, this time looking him in the eye. "O.K., I'll take the next test."

I picked the absolute worst time of year to take my first promotion exam in that non-air-conditioned hot box of a school. When I showed up that mid-July morning, the temperature outside was already in the mid-80s with 100 percent humidity. For Texas, it was looking like a typical dead-of-summer morning. To me, it was looking like a good day to drop dead from heat exhaustion in front of the Universe and all the spectators.

Midway through the exam, I was sure I'd float away in a rising creek formed by the stream of my own sweat. I didn't think it was such a cool thing now to be like puddle-sweaty Ron Hutto. Yet I trudged on and gave it my best. Although an uncomfortable, physically exhausting, and nerve-wracking experience, the exam was over in two hours and, according to examiners, I did well. While I didn't earn the higher-ranked blue belt; I wore yellow, and was ecstatic. That familiar sense of accomplishment and completion welled up in my body. The relief was overwhelming, and for the first time in a long time, I felt serene.

Slowly, my respect grew for Master Mike. A new love bloomed for the school and my classmates. An uncommon sense of peace emerged, the kind of calm that made me realize I'd never really been peaceful at all in the past. I just hadn't been depressed. This was true peace. By finally letting go of Kyoshi, I freed soul space to take on a new challenge, to see a new way, to explore a new art. To my prideful surprise, I hadn't really lost anything. The wisdom, skills, and inspiration that Kyoshi instilled were still there.

A Sore Spot

THE thing about martial arts is that, whether you're conscious of it or not, it gives you skills beyond kicking and punching that help snap you out of life's deepest emotional and mental difficulties. It gives you things like the courage to look deeply at every inner demon you possess and the strength to fight them all.

I began missing a lot of class because of a rarity: a new romance. The relationship didn't last long, though, and soon I was missing more class because of debilitating depression.

I was alone again, and I felt abandoned. I thought a lot about Daddy and how he left so easily when I was a kid. I didn't know what I was doing wrong; I just wanted to feel loved.

I didn't want to drink, but then again, I didn't want to do much of anything.

One day I shaved the hair on the tops of my feet as I'd done for years. (My hairy feet had bothered me since a roommate in college told me they were ugly and handed me a razor.) A few days later, I began obsessively plucking hair from the tops of my feet. It felt satisfying—one of the few things that made me feel better emotionally. It didn't take long for the obsession to move from removing hair from my feet to eliminating hair from my panty line. I plucked out every hair I could find with tweezers. It was a nightly ritual. The editor in me was relentless and thorough.

Soon, the plucked areas turned red. The relief I felt at plucking turned to shame, but I couldn't stop plucking. Feeling self-conscious about the sores on the tops of my feet, I avoided the taekwondo school.

Anxiety erupted at odd, inopportune times.

Repeatedly, I sat in my car at a stoplight a block from the school, chanting the mantra: *I'm going to class tonight. I'm going to class tonight.*

Just before the light turned green, I felt my chest tighten. I struggled to breathe. I feared I might faint and kill someone with my car.

Repeatedly, I turned the car around and headed back home. The farther I got from the school, the better I felt. By the time I got home, though, I was in full-blown shame.

Every night, I vowed I wouldn't pick at my sores, only to grab a pair of tweezers and resume my obsession. I wanted to feel good again, and I lost myself in trying to find satisfaction in my life through hairless feet.

I knew I had a problem, but I resisted seeking help.

One day on my way to the school, the anxiety attack at the stop light wasn't so bad, so I drove on and pulled into the school's parking lot. Once dressed and on the mat, I noticed Rich, an assistant instructor, in the corner of the room; custom demanded that I greet him with a bow.

Rich noticed my feet.

"Those look painful," he said of my sores.

I nodded, trying not to show any shame.

A long, uncomfortable silence followed.

"You need to take care of your feet," Rich finally said. "They're important."

"Yes, sir," I replied.

As had happened so often in the past, martial arts provided the tipping point.

The next day I sought a therapist.

The Only Constant Is Change

SOME alcoholics have the same sober mentor throughout their sobriety. Some martial artists have the same master throughout their training careers. Not me. Since Hilda moved to Michigan, I relied on several different sober mentors, and it was good because I was able to work through painful Daddy abandonment issues. In time, I accepted that people would come and go in my life and that it was vital that I let the yin and yang of relationships happen without resistance.

Therapy sucked, but unlike in college, I was awake for all my appointments. I took antidepressants as prescribed. My feet sores had healed. I could safely and confidently remove my socks without worry or embarrassment.

One night I went to the school to watch a black belt sparring class. I loved to watch sparring, but didn't like to participate myself; I wasn't a very good, fast, or elegant fighter. Sparring always brought up strange and strong emotions that I couldn't understand and would rather avoid. Instead, I sparred vicariously through the black belts as they "traded kicks," moving forward, backward, and sideways with the ease and finesse of ballroom dancers.

In a matter of minutes, my black belt buddy Brad plopped his thin body down on the bench beside me. He had bad and good news: Our grandmaster, Dr. Kim, had suffered kidney failure and could no longer handle the load of teaching taekwondo and judo at the University of Texas, plus run the business-end of a martial arts school. Dr. Kim turned over all UT classes and sold the school to a longtime friend and taekwondo colleague from Pensacola, Florida. This grandmaster held eighth-degree black belts in both taekwondo and hapkido and had been a taekwondo referee during the 1988 Olympic Games in Seoul, South Korea.

The grandmaster's résumé sounded great to my ears. From the facial expressions of the school's black belts, though, they weren't impressed. I sensed that few liked the idea of taking orders from a new master. For years before his failing health, Dr. Kim was seldom at the school anyway, preferring to leave Master Mike and the other black belts in charge of rank exams and basic instruction. Feathers were already ruffled, and pride was in danger of being swallowed, which in the martial arts big picture is a good thing unless the student who is about to be humbled gags while regurgitating his ego; I knew because I'd experienced the humble dry heaves myself.

After sparring, the black belts showered and stood around barefoot on the judo mat, waiting for Grandmaster. Though only a yellow belt, I was invited to stay for the meeting.

Wearing a drab, avocado-green polyester leisure suit, Grandmaster finally emerged from the school's office. I studied his tall, pencil-thin frame and his slow and graceful movement. He walked like a prince. His straight black hair was perfectly groomed, and he sported long sideburns. As he ordered everyone to sit in a circle on the judo mat, Grandmaster sat down in lotus position as easily as a feather falling gently to the ground. Then, as if he'd been in charge for years, he immediately appointed students to head committees for everything from public relations to first aid to tournaments. Everyone had a role, responsibility, and duty to the school, even me. I was in street clothes like everyone else. I thought he assumed I was one of the black belts. I felt honored.

Grandmaster, though, was no fool. He knew a wet-behind-the-ears martial artist when he saw one, and he immediately designated me "Water Girl."

"School mus' have bottle watah fo' students," he said in a thick Korean accent.

"Cah-ty, can you bring watah?"

"Yes, sir," I said, disappointed.

"Ah! Das good."

Grandmaster made it clear that this was his school now and changes were in order.

"School mus' be clean," he said. "It's ver impo'tant."

I looked around at the bloodstained judo mat and the dust-covered plaques and ceiling fans, and I had to agree. And while I wasn't sure what this man would be like as an instructor and mentor, I knew this: He was nothing like Kyoshi and Master Mike. He didn't scare me. He didn't intimidate me. More importantly, I had no illusions that he'd be the Master Po I'd always wanted.

Progress.

AS days turned into weeks, Grandmaster made good on his insistence that students keep the school sparkling clean. He considered cleaning a character-building exercise, and I actually enjoyed spending Saturday afternoons in the quiet of an empty school, dusting the plaques and trophies and cleaning bathrooms. But not everyone felt that way. Grandmaster encouraged all belt holders—including black belts—to do their part by taking out the trash, wiping down the mirrors, and vacuuming the mat. Everyone was expected to wear a clean, white uniform to class; ripped or torn pants and tops were not allowed, and belts had to be tied a particular way.

Grandmaster assumed we knew nothing. His first class involved several minutes of teaching everyone to sit down and stand up without using their hands for support.

Next, he insisted all students learn, understand, and give commands in Korean. He also expected students to adhere to formal school customs and rituals—kneeling in meditation (left knee down first and then the right) and practicing a series of bows. According to Grandmaster, just entering the training hall, stepping onto the training mat, and beginning class required three different bows. The trickiest custom was his insistence that students bow to him or other black belt holders immediately on sight. And when he said *on sight*, he meant it.

I was at a grocery store one morning on aisle 9 when I spotted Grandmaster on aisle 2. Good thing I was wearing my glasses or I might have seemed woefully disrespectful. Shoppers gave me strange looks as I immediately stopped in my tracks and bowed right in front of the "2 for $5" sale on Coca-Cola. I felt a little weird practicing one of our school customs out in the real world, but I couldn't avoid it; he saw me. Grandmaster stood patiently, almost regally, next to his grocery cart as I walked seven aisles to give him a more formal bow and greeting.

"Hello, sir," I said, bowing again.

"Ah, Cah-ty! How ah you?"

"I'm well, sir. Thank you. How are you today?"

"Grea'! Grea'! Ah, you live around here?"

"Yes, sir, not too far from here."

"Ah. Das good!"

Grandmaster got excited by the strangest things.

"Mmmm, O.K. I see you in class," he said.

"Yes, sir," I replied, bowing again as we each returned to our respective shopping.

Occasionally, Grandmaster sauntered onto the mat to fine-tune everyone's posture, stance, punches, and kicks.

"Good out-to-in middle block mus' come 45-deg'ee angle," he explained.

"Yes, sir!" students said.

"Kicks should explode: Pah!"

"Yes, sir!"

"You mus' focus."

"Yes, sir!"

"Nev-ah step back. Mus' always be positive. Step fo'ward. Pah!"

"Yes, sir!"

I thought Grandmaster was quirky, but the old black belts found nothing impressive or amusing about him whatsoever. They grumbled when he changed the forms we studied from the traditional *Palgweas* to the more modern *Taegeuks*. That meant everyone—black belts included—had ten new forms to learn, and students couldn't promote unless they knew all the forms up to their present rank.

Oddly, I didn't complain. For once, I listened to everyone else complain. I loved forms. I loved the focus, controlled breathing, balance, and coordination necessary to do these choreographed, multiple-attacker fighting sequences, so I didn't mind learning new ones.

What I didn't like were the push-ups that went with failing to relearn the new forms quickly enough.

It was rare when Grandmaster observed forms training in class. So I got a little jittery when he walked out on the mat. He always had something new to point out that I was doing wrong, and it hurt my fledgling confidence and my poor little feelings.

One day my classmates and I had butchered a form so nicely that the mere sight of us made Grandmaster moan.

"Let dem do ten push-up when dey make mistake," Grandmaster told Andrew, the lead instructor.

"You heard him," Andrew said.

My classmates and I hit the mat and began pumping out our punishment on our knuckles.

Apparently, we weren't respectful enough.

"Nah, nah," Grandmaster interrupted. "Let dem count out loud and 'Sir!' after each one."

"You heard him," Andrew said.

My classmates and I groaned as we hit the ground again and in unison chanted, "One, sir. Two, sir. Three, sir...."

Grandmaster interrupted again, shaking his head disapprovingly: "Mmmm, mus' be loud-ah. Try 'gain."

Louder now, we started over: "One, sir! Two, sir! Three, sir! Four, sir! Five, sir! Six, sir! Seven, sir! Eight, sir! Nine, sir! Ten, sir!"

I hated push-ups. My upper body had never been strong. My strength was in my legs. I could break boards with a front kick, but I struggled to pump out push-ups from my knees. Distraction regarding how much I hated push-ups resulted in even more push-ups as the class moved on to *Taegeuk Sam Jang* and I moved on to more mistakes.

Down on my knuckles again: "One, sir! Two, sir! Three, sir! Four, sir! Five, sir! Six, sir! Seven, sir! Eight, sir! Nine, sir! Ten, sir!"

I rose to my feet perturbed by my imperfection.

Next form: *Taegeuk Sah Jang*—and more mistakes.

"One, sir! Two, sir! Three, sir!"

"Shit!" I said softly as I rose to my feet. My eyes lifted to see Grandmaster looking right at me, arms folded in judgment.

Profanity was not allowed.

I hit the floor: "One, sir! Two, sir! Three, sir!"

"Cah-ty, we gonna make you ver' strong!" Grandmaster called out. "Now, try 'gain."

"Yes, sir!" I replied, but in my mind, I was thinking, *Shit! Shit! Shit! I can't believe this shit! And I'm paying good money for this shit! I'm such a little shit! What the hell is wrong with me? I do these forms fine when he's not watching.*

As if he read my mind, Grandmaster yelled out, "Cah-ty, you mus' focus. Try 'gain."

By the end of class, my arms were achy, tired, and rubbery. I was so exhausted that I no longer cared which classmates did forms better than me or whether Grandmaster was watching. I was just thankful I could breathe and walk.

Grandmaster's strength-building drills were a bit weird. Some nights, he ordered the class to walk around in a circle on all fours like bears. Other nights, he'd have us squat down and walk like ducks.

"You goin' to get ver' strong," he smirked, as students from white belt to black waddled in circles, panting heavily, red-cheeked exhaustion showing on everyone's face. I immediately started obsessing that I was going to duck walk right into a heart attack.

After surviving each class, I showered, dressed, and sat on the benches to watch Grandmaster teach the advanced class. He was hardest on them, bordering on humiliating. He pulled the public spotlight card on students whenever he felt like they weren't giving their best, and he amped up the pressure during exams.

As a green belt during a promotion test, I was called up to the line with four others to perform blocks and punches. I executed two hand strikes with as much power as I had, but something was missing. The strikes didn't feel quite as strong. Then I remembered: *I'm not yelling my* kihap *on each strike.*

Neither was anyone else.

I corrected my mistake going forward, yelling on each strike as loud as I could, but it was too late. Grandmaster stopped us before we moved on to the next hand technique and ordered all four of us to stand at the threshold of the open garage doors and face the neighborhood.

"*Kihap* ver' impo'tant. Now, *kihap* twenty time loud as you can. *Shishak*," he said, giving the command in Korean to begin.

I yelled as loud as I could, or at least I thought I did.

"Loud-ah. Try 'gain," Grandmaster said. We all yelled twenty more times, louder this time.

"Still nod loud enough. You have to make a big noise. Pah! Now! Try 'gain."

We yelled twenty more times, and I was as loud and roared with as much heart as ever. My neighborhood-waking *kihap* began to sound like a wounded seal. Grandmaster still didn't think it was loud enough.

After we finished our third round of *kihaps*, an eerie silence hung in the room. Everyone was still. The only noise came from barking neighborhood dogs. I was sure they were mocking us.

"O.K. Sit down," Grandmaster finally said, ordering us back to our seats on the dojo floor.

He didn't allow us to finish demonstrating the remaining techniques and gave us all Cs for that portion of the test.

That wasn't the last time Grandmaster put students in an uncomfortable and unexpected spotlight before examiners and spectators. During the oral portion of a December promotion exam, I was prepared to expound upon the meaning of taekwondo, explain the history behind the creation of my form, and cite the elements necessary to break a board.

Instead, Grandmaster wanted to know my favorite holiday song.

"*A Christmas Song* by Nat King Cole," I said.

"Oh, that righ'?" Grandmaster said. "Umm, sing it now, please."

"Now, sir?"

"Umm, uh, yes, righ'. Can you do it?"

I sang the song in the shower that morning, but as I looked around at my classmates and the spectators, stage fright froze my muscles. I'd broken boards in front of this crowd before, but I'd never belted out a holiday classic. I didn't want to refuse Grandmaster, though, so I shrugged my shoulders and started singing.

While I didn't sound like a wounded seal, my singing was terrible. Classmates and examiners listened respectfully, their eyes widening at some points, and Okkie grinned a wide smile. He laughed at me all the time during tests. It was his annoying way of seeing whether he could break my concentration. I couldn't tell if the others' grins were a good sign until after I finished.

The room erupted in applause and whistles.

"I didn't know you could sing," a classmate in line whispered.

"I didn't either."

While I didn't know what the heck singing had to do with martial arts, for once, I didn't analyze it.

I passed the test.

That was good enough for me.

Body of Shame

I'VE always hated my body.

"Look how *big* you've gotten," extended-family members said to me when I was a kid.

They were remarking about my belly, not my height.

"Looks like you've put on a little weight!" aunts would say.

Other family members teased me about my wide hips.

I believed them. Every word. And I became ashamed of my body.

One day in junior high sewing class, my teacher asked me why I chose a dress pattern for a chubby person.

"You're not chubby," she said.

I shrugged my shoulders in doubt.

I hated junior high gym class. All the girls changed clothes in front of one another. I heard classmates criticize others' bodies, and I was sure they were laughing at me.

The first time I stepped into the taekwondo school dressing room, I silently hyperventilated. The women's room reminded me of junior high. Except for a thin curtain between the door and the dressing room, the room was open. No individual changing rooms. No curtains. No privacy. Just a wall full of lockers and a shower.

Before class, I'd wait until the room was empty before changing into my uniform, cutting it real close to being late for the bowing-in ceremony every time. But I didn't want anyone to see my body.

After class, as the women headed to the dressing room, I took my time getting off the mat, hoping the room would clear before I went in to change. Sometimes I couldn't avoid it. I'd find many of them chatting in various stages of dress. The women didn't seem to care that they only had a bra and panties on while they made small talk about the movie they saw the night before or the guy they were dating. I always averted my eyes, pretended to organize my locker, and waited for the dressing room to empty before I changed clothes.

There are only so many times you can rearrange a one-square-foot locker before people start to think you're strange. I began engaging in light conversation, averting my eyes, and turning my back to the women as I quickly stripped off my uniform, then slipped on shorts and a T-shirt.

I didn't understand how these women could stand there half-dressed and carry on normal conversations. I was so embarrassed and uncomfortable it hurt.

In time, I realized that this was just something women did. And I began to think that maybe it was something I could do too without so much shame.

Someday, anyway.

LIZ was an important teacher.

I always threw clothes over my sweaty body and went home to shower.

Not Liz. She showered after every class.

And there she stood in front of me—naked—talking about how she blocked a great kick or punch in class, or how she was tired of the chauvinistic attitude of some of our male classmates.

She stood there for long seconds at a time, comfortably chatting. There wasn't one stitch of clothing on her body. There wasn't one bit of body shame.

I wondered how Liz did it.

I wanted to be like Liz.

It took years.

It took many tiny steps that began with me talking to someone without my uniform top. Then without my pants. It took years to develop a body image strong enough to change clothes in front of other women without excruciating discomfort. It took even more years to be able to take a shower, for that guaranteed that at some point I'd have to be naked. One day I braved undressing and quickly darting into the shower, and then darting out with a super-sized towel wrapped around my body. But I did it. The next time I took a shower wasn't easier. But slowly, it did become bearable.

I don't know when things changed for me, but one day I found myself talking to a new student about the kick I gave to a black belt's head in sparring and noticed that she had turned her back to change.

And I was naked.

And I was O.K. with it.

I still thought I was fat. I still hoped that someday I'd have the ultra-thin body of a super-strong black belt. But Liz planted the tiniest seed of body image self-esteem day after day in the women's dressing room. And after more time passed, it wasn't that I didn't think I was fat, but I just didn't care anymore.

YEARS later, I showed my mom a photo of me breaking a stack of pine boards with the blade of my hand. I was so proud of that photo. It showed me smashing the atoms of those boards—with coins, used as spacers and photographic effect, flying in the air.

Mamma had never seen me practice martial arts. I was excited to show her evidence of my work.

"That uniform sure makes you look fat," she said.

I shook my head and never showed her any martial arts-related photos again.

Sparring Ghosts

AS a mid-thirties woman with nine years of sobriety and eight years of martial arts training under my red belt, I still had many mysteries to solve and spiritual lessons to learn. Of all the challenges I faced in my life—work, sobriety, relationships—the one that continued to push my buttons and kick my butt was martial arts. More than anything else, martial arts made me deal head-on with fear.

Every damn day.

Every day, though, I continued suiting up and showing up for class. I still dreaded running. But more than anything, I hated sparring. After all the years of training, I still hated getting hit—and I still got hit. And I was still paying good money for it.

More and more, going to sparring class felt like trudging a lonely path down death row to the gas chamber. To get the coveted black belt, I had to put in my time in the sparring ring. I could never shake the sensation, though, of feeling like a vulnerable, weak, and bleeding perch about to be tossed into a pond of piranhas. After several two- to three-minute rounds, like clockwork, I couldn't breathe, ran out of gas, got sloppy and slow, and was then efficiently and effectively hammered by my opponents. Senior black belts with the endurance of Greek marathon runners were not the only ones kicking my white pants. The lowest-ranking students were beating the tar out of me too because by this point, no matter who I was sparring, I ended up mentally, emotionally, and physically crumbling. Nervous sensations spiked through my body like epileptic seizures. Muscles tensed. I felt six years old again, curling up into a ball, cowering in a corner in fear, my arms wrapped around my head. I stopped trying to fight back. Mentally, physically, and spiritually, I gave up, hoping that my surrender would end the pounding.

During breaks in sparring class, I watched my classmates fight, and I'd wonder how they did it. They looked so graceful, quick, powerful, and in control. I wondered if they had always fought so well. I wondered if I would ever fight well.

On a good day, fear still lurked in my shadow self: the dreadful, powerless, and helpless thought of not being able to defend myself in an attack. I made myself believe that all this sparring practice wouldn't hurt should I ever have to fight off an attacker one day. Most days, though, my sparring fears remained debilitating and paralyzing.

By this time in my training, I'd recognized that everyone had demons to fight and that my biggest demon was fear. This demon materialized most often during sparring practice—and whenever Okkie was around.

Okkie was the essence of a thin, fluid, flexible, and fast kicking machine. He thrived on inventing new ways to smack his foot in your face. Although arrogant at times, Okkie also was the most patient yet demanding sparring teacher, always there to gently push me a little harder to be a little faster, to spar a little longer. Kyoshi would have liked Okkie.

My mentor was committed to helping me find and correct every sparring weakness, either through trial and error or via embarrassment and humiliation. Okkie had a lot of material to work with. Once I donned the protective and bulky sparring gear—the dorky-looking, red-padded helmet; an awkward, clear-plastic mouth guard; a perspiration-producing chest protector with red-and-blue circled targets; and pull-on cloth forearm and shin guards that always felt like they were slipping off—I looked like the Pillsbury Doughboy. With all that gear, I felt five pounds heavier and moved with the speed of a tortoise.

"How does anyone expect me to fight in this?" I whined as classmates tied my chest protector. "God, I hate this crap!"

The source of irritation had more to do with the fact that I felt trapped against a wall with no escape. I never understood why sparring always pushed major panic buttons. Logically, I knew none of my classmates wanted to kill, maim, or hurt me, but I still always sensed that I was about to enter hell and never emerge. Blood gushed through my veins. Adrenaline surged. I was in primal survival mode. If I was lucky and centered enough, I'd remember to pray before entering the Olympic-sized ring:

God, please protect my classmates and me from harm or injury. And God, please help me survive this. Because I just know I'm going to die—and I'm not ready to die yet.

ON a cool Friday night in September, I suited up and was as mentally, physically, and spiritually ready to spar as the last time I got my butt kicked.

Okkie was there as usual.

He stepped up as my first opponent, grinning widely. His brown eyes read my apprehension like a dog reads fear in a postal worker. I loved him and hated him most during these few seconds before the instructor gave the order to spar.

"*Cha ryut*," the instructor said, giving the order to stand at attention.

"*Kyungrye*," the order to bow.

"Fighting stance, *Joonbe*."

Okkie and I released our respective yells, letting each other know we were ready to fight. Okkie moved his left leg forward, his foot turned in about thirty degrees. His right leg quickly shifted back, the ball of his foot slightly bobbing off the cushioned judo mat—his whole body ready to pounce on me as soon as he heard the order to begin: "*Shijahk*."

I marveled at Okkie's abilities. Graceful and relaxed, he fought in a seemingly effortless manner, preferring to evade strikes rather than block. As the match began, we danced around each other for a moment before he came in hard with a lightning-fast front kick.

"Hole," he said, pushing the ball of his foot squarely in my left floating rib. The hit wasn't as painful to my rib as it was my pride.

"Good shot," I nodded, covering up.

Now he waited. Okkie was patient. He knew that I'd come at him with a combination of kicks to defend my dinged ego. I threw a side kick and a roundhouse kick, missing both shots by inches. Okkie intuitively knew exactly how far to retreat to avoid getting hit. He quickly countered.

"Hole," he said, the ball of his foot gently pressing against my left floating rib.

I grunted under my breath.

"You're wide open there. Every time," Okkie said. "And I'm just gonna keep hitting you there until you block it."

He came in again, again, and again.

"Hole."

"Hole."

"Hole."

I let out another frustrated grunt through my mouth guard and tried another attack: A front kick and a roundhouse kick, followed by a solid punch over his guard and down hard to the chest. I finally scored a point.

Okkie rubbed his chest, smiling. He never wore a chest protector.

"That hurt," he finally said.

"You taught me that move," I said.

"I know. And I'm starting to wish I hadn't."

I was glad he had. My punches were my best chance to score. Standing short and stocky, I've never had the ideal leg reach for taekwondo. To get past most opponents' leg reach, I had to attack and quickly retreat. I'd never been fast. Hence, I got knocked around a lot. That's why I learned to take my punching victories, however small or seemingly insignificant, wherever and whenever I could.

I knew it was getting close to the two-minute mark because my energy was waning. And as usual, Okkie was there—patiently waiting.

"Hole," Okkie said, pressing his foot into my ribs a little harder now. He shook his head and grinned. "You're *still* wide open."

I sighed in exhaustion and frustration. Every move now was sluggish and slow. I wanted to quit. But I didn't, because even though I was no longer in Kyoshi's school, I remembered that damn "Don't Quit" sign. Okkie kept clobbering me with spinning crescent kicks to the head, and I kept taking hits. His kicks weren't hard, but they were right on target, and the force of the impact knocked my helmet-padded skull from side to side like a windshield wiper.

"You O.K.?" Okkie asked.

"I'm good," I said, adjusting my helmet so that I could see again. He hit me so easily, and I was embarrassed and ashamed that I had become so tired I couldn't simply get out of his way.

"*Goman!*" the instructor yelled, signaling the end of the match. That word was magical to me.

Okkie and I bowed to each other and shook hands.

"You hit me hard that time," Okkie said, smiling and still rubbing his chest.

"You taught me well," I replied.

Ripping the chin strap loose in frustration, I yanked off my helmet, pulled out my saliva-lathered mouthpiece, shook the sweat from my hair, and stepped out of the sparring ring for one round. It was my turn to protect my sparring classmates from smashing into the mirrors. As I guarded the mirrors, I watched a classmate take a hard hit to the chest. The sound of his groan reminded me of a despairing moan I used to make while getting smacked around as a child by my cousins.

It was a time I'd forgotten, and now the memories came back in a flash flood.

DURING my family's many visits to Llano, Texas, Mamma and her siblings gathered in Aunt Louise's dining room for penny-ante poker. They were serious card players, and none could concentrate with kids running around. One by one, all the children were ushered outside. The dining room door was closed and locked behind the last child out.

Slam.

Click.

To my six-year-old ears, these were the sounds of doom and dread, for now my sisters and I were vulnerable—at the mercy of our three male cousins' taunting and torture. I claimed my usual spot nearest the front door, sitting on the steps, elbows on knees, resting my chin in the palms of my hands, sighing, and dreading the inevitable.

Here it comes, I moaned, then held my breath and braced for the attack.

My three male cousins circled me like sharks—screaming, teasing, and laughing. Then at different intervals, they each came in for a hit.

Punch. Right in the shoulder.

Pop. Right in the head.

Slap. Right in the ear.

The pang from their punches always spurred a stinging sensation in my nose, a knot in my throat, and tears in my eyes. I took the hits with the quietest of whimpers, swallowed hard, put my head down deep into my knees, and tried not to look like I was crying.

I hated being out in that yard. I had nowhere to escape, no choice but to continue taking hits. I didn't know how to defend myself. If I fought back, the boys would just hit harder.

My cousins circled my sisters and me, trying to prove that Llano country boys were tougher than sissy girls from San Antonio. They were tough, indeed. They trotted barefoot and carefree in the summertime on hot pavement and sticker-covered yards, proudly pinned a huge diamondback rattlesnake skin above the bed in one of their rooms, and spent summer afternoons diving off different spots into the Llano River, neither knowing nor caring about the depth of the water. They were tough, small-town boys who loved to make sissy city girls cry. I did my best acting in that yard, trying to hide my tears. If they knew I was crying, they'd think I was a wounded animal, and next time, they'd come in for the kill. I rolled my little body up into a tight, tense ball, wrapped my arms around my head, held back the tears, and prayed for that magical sound.

Click.

Squeak.

That angelic noise—the sounds of Mamma unlocking and opening the door—changed my life in an instant. It gave me immediate relief, a safe home plate to slide into, and hope that maybe next time the beatings wouldn't happen, that someone would listen to me, believe me, protect me. Maybe next time I would be bigger, stronger, braver, and tougher.

109

I popped up from my perch on the front steps and rushed through the door to safety. Now I could breathe. Now I was safe. Now I could tell Mamma what happened out in the yard and she would demand retribution from my abusive cousins.

"Mamma, they hit us. They hit us real hard," I pleaded, rubbing my still-stinging shoulders.

Her reply was always the same.

"They're just being boys."

Mamma and her siblings argued to their death that they never locked that door, but my sisters and I—who rarely agree on any-thing—all remember they did. The door didn't have to be locked, though; my sisters and I knew better than to come into a house after Mamma ordered us outside. The whupping we received from our cousins was nothing compared to the beating Mamma would dish out for disobeying her. Hence, without the possibility of Mamma's protection, the penny-ante poker trauma drama was destined to be reenacted many more times. I never got used to being hit, and I was never rescued.

No wonder I hate sparring.

"MIRRORS!" I yelled as my sparring classmates neared the wall.

So it wasn't just crazy me after all. There was a reason behind why I felt as if I were going to die every time I sparred.

"*Goman!*"

Another sparring match was over. One more round and I'd be back in again.

As the next round began, another memory emerged.

WHEN I was nine years old, I dragged my feet every day on the half-block walk home from elementary school. I knew Barbara was going to be at my house when I got home. Mamma babysat eight-year-old Barbara while her mother worked afternoons. Barbara was mean, spoiled, and had a penchant for pinching me on the arm. I told Mamma about Barbara's pinching, but Mamma ignored me.

The pinching continued until one day in the backyard I gathered enough courage to stand up to Barbara.

"Stop it!" I said.

"Or what?" she replied, pinching me again.

This time I returned her pinch.

Barbara wailed as if I'd broken her arm. Mamma came blazing out the back door, running to Barbara's rescue. Mamma ordered me to say I was sorry. I wasn't, and I didn't. That's when Mamma gave me the look of death, and I knew I'd get a fierce whipping later that night.

Barbara, who had long stopped crying, stood in Mamma's shadow and smiled a wide, satisfied grin.

That night, right after a Last Supper-like dinner I couldn't enjoy, Mamma calmly ordered me to lay my body over the edge of my bed and began whipping me with Daddy's leather belt. It hurt, and I felt like crying, but I wasn't going to let Mamma know I was in pain. I swore to myself that I wasn't going to give her the satisfaction of seeing me cry. Mamma swung the belt harder, yet I remained silent. I accepted my punishment in as comfortable a numbness as my young body could attain.

I never cried again.

So that's when I stopped crying.

"MIRRORS!" I yelled as one of my classmates came close to the edge of the mat.

"Goman!" the instructor yelled.

It was my turn to fight again.

I pulled my helmet on and reattached the chin strap. My mouthpiece was in place and my breathing under control. I was as ready as ever to face this new realization. I rejoined the ranks, bowed to another black belt opponent, and said a quick prayer:

God, please help me remember that these people are not Barbara.

I won't get in trouble for fighting back.

And my classmates aren't my cousins.

They're not my cousins.

They're not my cousins.

Another round began. Not ten seconds passed before I again became tense.

"Look at his eyes, not his chest," one classmate coached.

111

"Keep moving around," another said. "Don't just back up, move in circles. Use your sparring footwork!"

"You're too tense. Relax!"

I took my eyes off my opponent for a split second to leer in frustration and irritability at the hecklers. I couldn't do everything everyone was recommending.

"You'd be tense, too, if you were about to get pummeled!" I snapped.

"Relax your shoulders!" someone yelled. "You're using up all your energy being tense."

Despite the earlier epiphany, sparring remained as difficult as ever. Tense, tight muscles still hampered my maneuverability and flexibility, making me slow and tired. I tried to relax, and for a while my technique improved. I landed better, cleaner shots and was fluid enough to evade my opponent's advancing kicks. Eventually, though, I'd receive a solid shot—to the head, solar plexus, or ribs—and the old defenses kicked in. Shields up. I tensed. I braced. I forgot to breathe. I became winded, slow, and sloppy all over again. If any good was coming of this beating, it was that I became convinced it was time to start jogging with my new friend at Camp Mabry's track. I had to build endurance. I had to outlast my opponent. I had to learn to fight smarter and not spend so much energy on techniques that didn't work. I had to make new, more positive memories. But until then, I prayed for that magical word.

"*Goman!*"

"Thank you, God," I whispered between exhaustive breaths, my body bent over, palms resting on my knees.

Out of the corner of my eye, I saw Grandmaster step onto the mat and walk toward me. He often secretly watched class through his office window. Something must have caught his eye, because by the way he was looking at me, I knew he wasn't going to ask me to sing.

"Cah-ty, you tired?" Grandmaster asked.

"Yes, sir. Oh, I mean, no, sir!"

"Ah, das good," he said, smiling. "Cah-ty, when you spar, you mus' move back jus' once. Unde'stand?"

"Yeah, ye-, yes, sir!"

"When you step back one time, then two time, you say to your opponent: 'Please kill me.' Unde'stand?"

"Yes, sir!"

"O.K. Good job," he said, pumping his fist with a satisfied grin.

He wants me to fight back, I thought. *And he's going to watch me from now on to make sure I do. Great. That's just great.*

I ripped the chin strap from my helmet in disgust and peeled off my sweat-drenched gear. Although I had survived one more sparring class unbruised and unhurt, I still felt frustrated and embarrassed at my lack of sparring ability. I sat on my knees in meditation with the rest of the class, hoping for a little inspiration as sweat trailed down my forehead and into my eyes. I felt defeated. I wanted to cry. I knew that I needed to get past this hurdle if I expected to get a black belt. Now that I knew why I'd always hated getting hit, and hesitated to hit back, now what? What was it going to take for me to finally fight back? To really fight back?

Cathy Chapaty

Part V

The Final Rites of Passage

Cathy Chapaty

On Being Humbled

I avoided Dr. Hill's morning class much like I used to tiptoe around Mamma. A tall, thin, bespectacled, gray-haired, fifth-degree black belt with a million years' experience in martial arts, Dr. Hill had a reputation for being a tough teacher.

Black belts encouraged me to attend his early morning class, especially since I was on the verge of promoting to the first of two black stripes. It was an important mark; I would finally surpass the red belt level I reached with Kyoshi.

But like Mamma, Dr. Hill scared the hell out of me.

I resisted for months, and then one day at 6:30 a.m., I put my petty fear of authority figures aside.

I drove into the school's dimly lit parking lot at the same time he did.

"That's not Cathy Chapaty, is it?" he said, squinting through his glasses. The sun had not yet risen.

"Yes, sir," I replied, grabbing my gym bag out of the trunk of my car and hoisting it over my shoulder.

"Well, fancy meeting you here. You're not here to work out, are you?"

"Yes, sir, I am."

"Well, that's great!"

I can understand his shock. I'd trained at the school for about four years without ever attending his morning class. A night owl, I was even shocked that I had rolled out of bed that early and that easily to train.

Having suited up, I offered the customary bow to the flags, and stumbled onto the floor. The mat was cold. The air was crisp. It was quiet, still, and serene. There were no other students bustling and chatting before and after workouts, no phones ringing, and no one coming in or out of the office door. It seemed wonderful and at the same time eerie and uncomfortable, as if a thunderbolt was about to boom.

Dr. Hill emerged from the men's locker room, followed by Walter, a green belt. The three of us bowed in as a class, and Dr. Hill began a nice, slow head-to-toe warm-up. We rotated our heads and then our shoulders. We leaned our right arm to the left, our left arm to the right. Hip rotations. Body rotations. Knee rotations. Ankle rotations. Then we swung our legs forward, backward, and to the side.

"Let's run in rank," Dr. Hill said.

He led us in a slow trot, using every inch of the mat. I was relieved with the pace, for I still had menacing fears of dropping dead of an aneurysm if I pushed the pace too hard. I was keeping up with Dr. Hill well, but Walter was right behind me.

Dr. Hill never quickened the pace. Instead of running a few quick laps, we ran a lot of slow ones. A whole lot. I managed to keep up without cheating and cutting corners as we circled the mat, but I was getting winded. My thighs felt like cement blocks. Dr. Hill finally ordered us to stop running and line up again, yet reminded us to keep moving. Without stopping, we went right into jumping jacks.

Oh, God, I thought between shortened breaths, *God, help me. God, help me. God, help me.*

"Stay with me," Dr. Hill ordered.

The jumping jacks drill was not just a cardiovascular exercise, but a lesson in using your peripheral vision. Instructors would speed up the pace, then s-l-o-w down, and then speed up again. Today, I was grateful for jumping jacks, because I was concentrating so much on trying to maintain the proper speed that I didn't pay much attention to the fatigue. Eventually, my gas tank emptied. We finally stopped jumping, and I came to a complete, winded halt, sucking major air and feeling a tinge of regret.

I should have slept in this morning.

Dr. Hill moved on quickly to basic punching drills.

Oh, good. I'm good at this, I assured myself.

First technique: high block. Dr. Hill demonstrated the technique and then stepped back to watch how well Walter and I could thrust our fleshy forearms above our heads. Dr. Hill wasn't happy with my technique. He picked up a padded bat and stood directly in front of me. I immediately felt very small and scared.

"Agaaaain," Dr. Hill instructed.

As if jarred in molasses, I slowly and sloppily lifted my left forearm up across the top of my head as Dr. Hill slammed the bat square over my skull.

Whack.

The impact stung. I fought the urge to rub the top of my head.

"Too late," Dr. Hill said. "You've got to bring your arm up fast. And it should be at an angle. Your arm is too flat across the top here."

He spent a few seconds adjusting my block to where it should be.

"Agaaaain," he ordered.

Once more, I tried to block the fast and hard downward strike of the foam bat. Once more, I got whacked.

"No, no, no!" he said, a little more frustrated. "You've got to be faster. Again."

Same technique, same result. This time, however, I wasn't whacked as hard, a more properly placed forearm absorbing the blow. He only tapped me on the head this time.

"That's better," he finally said. "Are you left-handed or right-handed?"

"Left-handed, sir," I answered.

"That's what I thought. You're obviously better on your left side. O.K., keep trying."

Dr. Hill took his bat and stood before Walter.

God, help that poor boy.

Surprisingly to my bruised ego, Walter did just fine.

Now Dr. Hill moved on to an outer middle block. He put the padded bat away, grabbed a bamboo stick, and walked over to face me.

My throat was in knots. I knew I wasn't going to like this drill at all.

"Begiiiin," he ordered.

Before I could deflect the stick away from my body, he poked me in the chest.

"Too late," he declared. "Agaaaain."

Poke.

"Still too late. Faster. Agaaaain."

Poke.

Poke.

Poke.

I growled aloud in frustration and self-hatred. I was a red belt, and I couldn't even get a simple, basic blocking technique right. Not yet having my first cup of coffee was no excuse. What if someone actually attacked me out on the street with a knife—not a harmless bamboo stick, but a real, deadly weapon. Would I be able to protect myself? Apparently not, I concluded.

"Still too slow," Dr. Hill said. "Once again. You've got to be faster."

The next time I was able to block the stick enough that it only brushed my shoulder.

"Better," Dr. Hill said, moving on to Walter.

A huge sigh left my tense body. I felt defeated and discouraged, and negative self-chatter that hadn't entered my psyche in months returned full force.

You have no business wearing a red belt.

And you want to be a black belt someday? No way.

What are you thinking? Who do you think you are anyway?

If you can't do these basic techniques, you have no business wearing a black belt around your waist. It would just be a lie.

My self-confidence and pride were crushed. I wanted to cry, but I couldn't.

Dr. Hill now ordered Walter and me to move to the center of the mat and begin trading kicks, a drill meant to build accuracy, coordination, and balance, and to improve strategy. I hated mock sparring as much as I hated getting bonked on the head with a padded bat and poked in the chest with a bamboo stick. But the clock told me there were only fifteen minutes of class time left, so I told myself I could do this. I could muddle through.

Although tense the whole time, I sparred well. Still, knots remained in my throat, and I was on the verge of tears. I continued holding back my emotions as Dr. Hill coached us on our sparring and pushed us to speed up the pace.

"Use that back kick, Cathy. That's a good kick for you," he said.

I did and landed a solid, gentle hit to Walter's solar plexus.

"Good!" Dr. Hill commended.

For the moment, a little bit of self-esteem returned.

"You're not turning your hip over far enough on that side kick, Cathy."

"Yes, sir!"

"Turn your hip!"

"Yes, sir!"

I did and gently pressed the blade and heel of my foot just below Walter's floating ribs.

"Better," Dr. Hill praised.

"Thank you, sir."

Walter sparred well, too, and for a while, we were in a nice rhythm.

Dr. Hill began a traditional warm-down exercise: push-ups from the knees, using the two protruding knuckles. It was an uncomfortable position for my hands, and it seemed as if we did push-ups for an eternity. My arms began to wobble in exhaustion and, in a flashback from that day with Master C, I feared Dr. Hill would grab the back collar of my uniform and force-feed my face to the mat.

When we finally finished, I felt as if Mamma had just unlocked the door and saved me from my cousins.

We ended class just as customarily as we began, bowing to Dr. Hill once more. I thanked him for his time and then quickly bolted to the dressing room. My eyes began to water.

Some red belt, I thought.

I hung my head as I grabbed my things and ashamedly left the building without saying another word.

I cried all the way to my running buddy's house. Marianna silently watched as I cried for an hour on the edge of her sofa.

I couldn't believe that after all the years of martial arts training, after all the struggles and hours of hard work, after all this time I couldn't even defend myself against a padded bat and a simple bamboo stick.

Marianna, who was quickly becoming my greatest fan, let me cry for as long as I wanted. She asked if she could help.

"No," I said amid a trail of teardrops and snot. "I just thought I was better than that. I thought I could do it, defend myself, that's all."

"You can, Cathy," she reassured. "You're just not used to training with all those bats and sticks. You didn't expect it."

"But what if he was a stranger on the street and he had a real knife?" I cried, sucking air between whimpers. "I'd be dead right now."

"You don't know that. In fact, I'm sure your reaction time would be a lot different, a lot faster if he really did have a knife."

"Yeah, I would've just run!" I said, finally letting out a little laugh. "It's just that I've never just wanted to wear a black belt. I've always wanted to *be* a black belt. And I just didn't think I was one today."

"Uh, could that be because you're *not* a black belt yet?"

"Smart-ass."

Marianna smiled.

After a moment of silence, I looked up to see her now familiar and extremely annoying look of expectation. An avid soccer player, Marianna grew up playing all sorts of team sports. To stay in shape, she ran several times a week at either Lady Bird Lake or the track at Camp Mabry. Earlier that year, she competed in her first triathlon. She was sports-minded. One of her favorite movies was *Rocky*. I knew she wasn't going to let me give up.

"So, are you going back to Dr. Hill's class again?" she quizzed.

"No! I don't want to go back there. He's mean!" I cried.

"He's not mean. He's good. He can teach you a lot. And I think it would be good for you to go back regardless of how poorly you think you did today."

"I know," I stubbornly sighed. "I'll go back next week."

"Good," she said.

"Yeah, good for you. No one's trying to give your chest bruises with a bamboo stick."

"Hey," she said as she gathered her things for work, "I'm proud of you."

"Thanks," I said nodding in half-acceptance.

Freeze or Fight?

I'M barefoot, walking home from the school. It's late. Dark. I decide to take a shortcut through a building, and then through an unlit stairwell. It gets darker the farther down the stairwell I go. I know it's not a safe place to be alone at night. I decide not to take the shortcut after all and begin climbing back up the stairs when the Lurking, Waiting One appears. He's big—a towering male with clean-cut, blonde hair. He wants to rape me.

I look into his eyes. I sense he has bad intentions and I know I'll have to use what I've learned in taekwondo—or die. I'm scared, but I know I have to fight. I only hope my training has been thorough enough to help me get out of this situation alive.

Before either of us makes a move, an Angel dressed in street clothes suddenly emerges from the bottom of the stairwell, and without him saying a word, I sense he wants me to walk with him. The Lurking, Waiting One steps to the side as I climb the stairs with the Angel toward the light of a parking garage. The Lurking, Waiting One follows us. We all emerge in the open, and I turn to thank the Angel for letting me walk with him to safety. But before I can say anything, the Angel turns to the Lurking, Waiting One.

"Boy, you're lucky I came along when I did," the Angel tells him. "She's a black belt, you know. She could'a really hurt you."

The Lurking, Waiting One's face drains to a powder white. He turns and quickly walks away. I'm baffled because when I turn to the Angel, I realize that he was not there to save me, but to protect the Lurking, Waiting One.

ANOTHER recurring dream. Even though I could break boards with the blade of my hand, I still wondered whether I could defend myself in an attack. As I rolled out of bed, I hoped to never find out.

It was a cool fall Sunday morning. I grabbed a cup of coffee from the neighborhood convenience store, then drove to a community center downtown. I was meeting members of my sober group to pick up trash around the perimeter of the building. It was our "rent" in exchange for the center allowing us to use one of its rooms for a weekly meeting.

I was early. None of the other members was there yet, and probably wouldn't be for a few more minutes. Deciding not to wait, I grabbed a few plastic grocery store bags from my trunk and started picking up garbage.

The city was quiet. Sunday in downtown Austin. Very few cars on the street. It was a nice change from the hectic weekday pace kept by state officials who worked near the Capitol or the staff who worked at the hospital up the street.

I was enjoying the solitude and silence. Then I spotted something strange out of the corner of my eye.

A small man yelled and waved at me from across the street. I looked up, but not recognizing him or understanding what he was saying, I returned to picking up trash. As soon as the traffic light changed, he crossed the street and trotted toward me, reaching his palm out for a handshake. I refused; my hands were already crawling with trash-borne bacteria.

Standing at about my height, he had a thin mustache and wore a green-hooded windbreaker, evergreen pants, and black boots. His most noticeable characteristic was an ominous teardrop tattoo below his right eye. My stomach sank. Growing up in San Antonio, I knew that the tattoo meant that he had either stabbed or shot a rival gang member, or been stabbed or shot himself. This was a bad dude.

"Do you have some spare change?" he asked. "I just got out of Brackenridge Hospital. I broke my finger."

He offered a loosely wrapped bandage on his right hand as proof.

"Hey, lemme help," he said before I could reply, reaching for one of the plastic bags. "I can help you."

"No, that's O.K.," I said, brushing his hand away. "I can't pay you to help me. I don't have any money. That's why I'm picking up trash. I'm just volunteering to do this."

"Oh," he said.

I thought once he realized he wasn't getting a handout, he'd leave me alone, yet he continued to stand there watching me pick up trash. It was becoming obvious he had no intention of leaving.

"Uh, you live around here?" he asked.

"Nope. Down south," I said, feeling increasingly uncomfortable.

"Oh," he said, pausing again. "What's your name?"

"Cathy," I said, continuing to pick up trash and avoiding eye contact. Maybe he'd see that I was busy and leave me alone.

"Oh. You married?"

"Nope," I said with a loud sigh, hoping he would get the hint that he was bothering me and leave.

"Oh. You got a boyfriend?"

Do I have a what?

I was appalled at his questions, and I wanted to snap at him, but my instincts told me to keep my reply polite:

"I'm seeing someone right now," I lied, continuing to pick up trash but now using the peripheral vision honed in martial arts class to keep him in my sights. I felt an ever-increasing degree of uneasiness. I hoped my sober group friends would show up soon.

"Lemme help you," he said again, approaching me closer this time.

"No. Really, that's all right," I said, quickly rising from my trash-picking stoop. "You don't have to help. Look, why don't you go home? You must be tired. You look like you need some rest."

I was sincere. He really did look a mess.

"No, I'm O.K.," he said, pausing again and looking down at the ground as if he were looking for something. Then he checked over his left and right shoulders.

"Uh, how much do you weigh?" he said, circling me and stopping at my left side.

Oh, shit.

I glanced downward, never letting him out of my peripheral vision. I had to be ready to fight. To my surprise, my body was already

ready: The whole time he was talking, my feet and hips had maintained a natural fighting stance.

"I'm gonna kiss you," he blurted, thrusting his body forward. I immediately dropped my trash bag.

"I think you need to leave," I said, stepping forward, jabbing him hard in the center of his chest with my forefinger and middle finger.

The minimal force of my two fingers was enough to push him back a couple of paces. I was flabbergasted by its impact and wondered if maybe he stumbled backward because he was drunk. He looked equally stunned, though, unsure of what just happened.

"Hey, what's the matter with you? I just like you. You're pretty," he said, flashing an eerie smile as he approached me again.

"I think you need to leave NOW," I said, stepping forward again.

This time, he suddenly backed away. He continued retreating as I stepped forward. Finally, he turned and walked away, all the while yelling, "Hey, what's the matter with you? You a lesbian or something?"

I kept my eye on him until he was out of sight, and then in a convulsion of post-anxiety relief, fright, and shock, I collapsed and fell to my knees on the cement pavement. I replayed the incident in my mind.

He could have had a knife.

He could have had a gun.

I could have overreacted and kicked him, punched him, made him really mad, and started a fight bigger than I could finish.

A sober friend finally drove into the center's parking lot.

"Hey, Caaaa-thy," my friend yelled in her familiar Texas twang.

I stood in the parking lot, unable to move. She sensed something was wrong.

"You O.K.?" she quizzed. "You're white, girl. You seen a ghost or what?"

"I think I was almost attacked," I said in matter-of-fact shock— the kind of crisis-mode calm that I had mastered throughout all those chaotic times with Daddy and Mamma.

My friend held the key to the building. I numbly followed her up the stairs to call the police.

When an officer arrived, I robotically regurgitated a description of the man. The officer frantically scribbled notes, then paused.

"I saw a man fitting this description loitering in the area earlier that morning," the officer said. "I'll cruise around to find him."

Stoic and professional, the officer offered me no more comfort than a warning to be more careful in certain parts of town at low-activity hours. I offered an understanding, shameful nod.

It was my fault. I should have waited for my friends.

After the officer left, I wandered into the sober meeting, sat down, and remained in a daze, trying to process what happened in that split second.

I'm so incredibly lucky.

Part of me didn't feel lucky, though. I felt angry. Nothing said during the meeting quelled my growing fury. I didn't know whether to be angry with myself or appreciative to the Universe for keeping me safe. I walked out at meeting's end irritable, restless, and discontent, bypassing offers for lunch and opting instead to go home to be alone with my confused and angry thoughts.

Instead, my car drove to the school; I still had a key from my Water Girl days.

The training hall was deserted. No one came to work out on Sundays. I had the place to myself.

Perfect.

For in addition to punching and kicking the big hanging bag, I needed to scream—loud. I donned my red boxing gloves and began pushing my body against the bag. I envisioned that man and remembered how appalled I was that he thought he had the right to kiss anyone he wanted. That he could just walk up and touch any woman on the street. That any woman would welcome his advances, and if she didn't, she had to be a lesbian.

Every time I hit that bag, I saw his face. I kicked and kicked, and then threw solid punches. I kneed the bag and threw strikes with the back of my fist with a force I'd never known. I thrashed the bag over and over until all I saw was a disorienting and blurring flurry of punches, kicks, and long, deep screams. I yelled until my throat began to hurt.

Within the safe bounds of that bag, I let out all my anger. At him. At myself. Why was I so nice to him? Why did I tell him my name, what part of town I lived? What was I thinking? Or *was* I thinking? Part of me wished he'd have pushed me or grabbed my arm, attacked me in a way that I'd have had no choice but to beat the crap out of him. I wanted to hurt him just like Grasshopper killed the emperor's soldier after the death of Master Po.

After about twenty more minutes, I was thoroughly winded and exhausted, too tired to be angry anymore. I fell to my knees on the soft judo mat, every pore of my body exuding sweat, my own Big Ron puddle soaking into the denim cloth.

As my breathing returned to normal, my mind started to clear. The anger subsided, and I was able to see that something good had actually come of this ugly incident:

I had defended myself.

I didn't cower.

I stood my ground.

When faced with a threatening situation, I didn't freeze. My Llano cousins and Barbara be damned: Little old me finally fought back. And endurance was never an issue.

I peeled off the sweaty red boxing gloves and studied my now-wrinkled fingers. Slowly, I pressed the two fingers into my chest, in the same spot I poked the man. A sharp pain ripped through my center.

I tried to remember where or when I'd learned that two-finger jab. Kyoshi didn't teach it to me. Master Pliska didn't either. I didn't remember Grandmaster or Okkie showing it to me. It just seemed to come—instinctively.

I'd come a long way since the Thanksgiving Day fiasco.

Progress, not Perfection

DESPITE a promise to return to Dr. Hill's class, I procrastinated. Weeks passed. I rationalized excuse after excuse to avoid any further damage to my ego.

Marianna, meanwhile, didn't say anything more. She just gave me "the look."

"Oh, all right," I said one day. "I'll go back. I just want to get this rank exam over with first. I need all the self-esteem I've got right now."

The rank exam came and went.

I passed.

It was time to shut up, suit up, and show up to Dr. Hill's class again. No more excuses.

About a month after the lesson in humility hell, there I was again, stumbling sleepy-eyed out of the house in the dark dawn of 6:30 a.m. for another early class.

God, please help me, I pleaded in prayer in my car before I killed the motor. With dread, I grabbed my gym bag. The school was dark and quiet when I arrived. Empty. I let myself in, turned on the lights, and suited up.

Still no Dr. Hill.

I bowed onto the mat and began warming up.

Still no Dr. Hill.

Maybe he won't show, I wished.

Just as the thought crossed my mind, I heard a vehicle pull into the lot and a door slam.

Dr. Hill, dammit.

As I continued warming up on the mat, I coached myself into a positive attitude.

It's probably not going to be as bad as you think.

Just relax and do the best you can.

"Hi," Dr. Hill said. "Glad to see you back again."

"Good to be back, sir," I lied.

"Well, it looks like it's just going to be you and me today, so why don't you just work on your own thing—unless you need my help. How's that sound?"

"That'll be fine, sir."

"O.K., then," he said, turning toward the locker room.

Yes!

I did a short internal happy dance. Now I could relax. No expectations. No poking and prodding bamboo sticks. No bats pounding my head. This was the kind of workout I favored: No pushing the limit.

I spent the first few minutes doing some warm-up kicks and then began practicing the techniques necessary for the next promotion. I was having a balance problem with the step-spinning-hook kick, and Dr. Hill offered to help.

He grabbed a target-kicking pad and ordered me to hit the mark, watching me lose my balance and miss. First, I kicked too high. The next time, too low. The kick felt awkward, ugly, and clunky. I knew I was doing something wrong but hadn't figured out what yet. I grunted in frustration again and again, then listened to Dr. Hill's insightful analysis. He spent a good chunk of time teaching me how to step into the kick.

"A lot of the evening instructors are missing the importance of this first step, and so you don't get your proper footing. If you don't have the proper footing, you'll lose your balance and be off target. That's what you're doing. Try it again, and this time make sure you have your footing correct."

"Yes, sir."

I followed his instruction, and it worked.

"Better!" he cheered. "Now, agaaaain."

Excited that I had just gotten the kick right, I didn't pay enough attention to my footing the next time. I lost my balance and missed the target.

"Aw, that was terrible," Dr. Hill said. "You're doing it again. Watch your footing."

The next time, I did better. And the next time. And the time after that.

"Good! Better."

"Thank you, sir. I needed someone to just pick this apart with. I knew it didn't feel right."

"Just keep working on your foot placement. It's not about being too slow. It's about having good balance. Step forward and settle before you kick."

The hour was over. We bowed to the flags and stepped off the mat. Before Dr. Hill disappeared into the locker room, though, I stopped him. Because I was still working my sober program, I had to be honest.

"You know, my last class here with you was really hard for me," I began.

"Oh, really?"

"Yeah. You opened my eyes as to how far I still have to go as a martial artist. But it was good—it was a good experience for me to go through. I needed it."

"Well, I'm glad you came back then."

"Me, too," I said truthfully this time.

We parted, and I left the school feeling a gentle, peaceful combination of humility and accomplishment—the kind of calm that I'd always imagined Grasshopper possessed. I didn't know how long the serene aura would remain, but I was glad that I had the opportunity to experience it, if only for a moment.

Back into the Fire

KYOSHI warned me: The final phase on the road to black belt is like going "back into the fire," when you review everything you thought you learned with greater intensity, and when mental, physical, and spiritual endurance would be tested.

I thought building physical endurance was going to be the biggest dragon in the next phase of my development. I conveniently forgot that Grasshopper had to mentally block the physical pain of moving that black cauldron away from the doorway. And that's a good thing, because had I known the mental hell I'd have to go through to become ready—to become a true black belt—I might have balked.

"Pick 'Em Up, Put 'Em Down"

PHYSICAL endurance training began in the fall of 1999 at Camp Mabry's dusty, one-mile dirt track. Marianna finally convinced me that running would build the endurance necessary for the final phase of my test: the sparring ring.

I trusted her.

Then I immediately began to hate her.

Marianna was born to coach. She knew exactly where my buttons were, and how hard to push them. I, on the other hand, was a born whiner. My character defects were still pretty glaring. I was scared, wimpy, and stubborn—afraid to run and at times determined not to run any faster or any farther than absolutely necessary to satisfy her. If it were up to me, we wouldn't even be out on that track. I wanted my black belt, I wanted the peace that Grasshopper had, but I hated running enough that, on my own, I'd probably take the test without trotting one inch.

Marianna ignored my grade-school-like, crybaby complaints and instead focused on the task at foot. She gently encouraged me to follow her lead.

"You can do it," she said one day as we ran. "I know you can do it. Have I told you how proud I am that you got out here and ran today?"

"No," I panted between breaths.

"Well, I am."

As we got to the quarter-mile mark, she again congratulated me on a nice start.

"Start?" I cried. "How far do you expect me to go?"

"All the way. Come on, just stay with me."

Stay with me. Those words were my Pavlov's dog heads-up for what was next. Marianna picked up the pace and challenged me like a drill sergeant to keep trudging forward.

"Pick 'em up. Put 'em down," she chanted. "Pick 'em up. Put 'em down."

I leered out the corner of my eye but tried my best to control my breathing, loosen the stitch in my side, and find some kind of rhythm to my run. I felt like a car wobbling from a blown-out tire. Every part of the run was a struggle. Still, one-quarter mile became a half-mile, and then a three-quarter mile. With every awkward and lunging step forward, I marked a personal best. With every step forward, though, I wanted to quit. That old familiar wall—where I felt afraid that if I didn't quit immediately I'd die right there in the dirt—shot up.

"I'll bet your mind is telling you to quit right about now," Marianna said.

"Can we?"

"No!" she barked. "Here's the part where you tell your mind to shut up."

"I know I'd like to tell someone to shut up," I mumbled.

Marianna simply grinned, her breathing perfectly controlled. She was enjoying her run, and it pissed me off.

"If you can do half a mile," she continued, "then what does that mean?"

"That's enough for today?"

"No!" she barked. "You can do half a mile more."

"I can do half a mile more, ma'am!"

"Great! And why do you want to do half a mile more?"

"I want my black belt, ma'am," I panted between breaths. "I want my black belt."

AFTER a few months of regular running, that one-mile jaunt around the track at Camp Mabry actually became comfortable, and, being proud of my accomplishment, I bragged to Marianna.

A mistake.

Marianna didn't think like me. If she went a good distance comfortably, she considered that not just an accomplishment, but also an indication that she could go farther. After my admission, she signed me up for a 5K run at Austin's Zilker Park. I grumbled, but I showed up for the Saturday morning race, determined to run the entire length without stopping no matter how slow.

I didn't get my feelings hurt when a costumed Indian chief on horseback trotted past me at Mile 1. And I didn't get flustered when a man in a racing wheelchair whizzed by. What hurt my pride the most was when the speed-walking grandmother, holding hands with her five-year-old grandson, left me in the dust.

Still, I kept running.

"I want my black belt," I panted. "I want my black belt."

Eventually, I crossed the finish line. I'd finished my first 5K race, running all the way. It was a turning point in physical and mental endurance.

Boo-Boos and Black Eyes

MIRACULOUSLY, I managed to make it through the many family trips to Llano with my punch-happy cousins without sustaining a single black eye. And I got through years of martial arts training with Kyoshi, Master Pliska, and Grandmaster without a blemish. Yet six months before my black belt test, I got popped in the face—twice.

Tye, one of the school's most ferocious fighters, stood just a bit taller than me and sported well-defined arms and legs that a body builder would envy. I didn't dread sparring Tye as much as Okkie, but I should have. One day, she slammed a crescent kick right into my temple. I didn't see it coming, which meant that I didn't block it.

"You gotta learn to keep your guard up, girl," the instructor said.

"Yes, sir," I said, holding ice to my eye.

Tye was remorseful.

"Cathy, I'm so sorry," she said.

"Don't be. I should have blocked it."

"Well, that's true."

The next day, I snuck into the office at the publishing company, ninja-snagged a plastic bag of ice, and hid in my cubicle with my face turned away from office traffic. Eventually, a co-worker popped into my cubicle to ask a question—and saw my shiner. For the rest of the day, a constant trickle of people from the editorial and advertising departments came by to see the bruise.

"Did you get that from breaking boards with your face?" colleagues joked.

"Very funny," I smirked.

Three months later, it happened again. This time, the injury came from a collision with a judo black belt's heel during self-defense drills.

The next day, I again snuck into the office, ninja-snagged a plastic bag of ice, and hid in my cubicle with my face turned away from office traffic. Again, a coworker eventually popped into my cubicle and saw my shiner. For the rest of the day, folks in the editorial and advertising departments came by to see the newest bruise.

"You're almost a black belt, right?" a colleague asked.

"Yes," I mumbled in humiliation.

"So, that's not supposed to happen at your level, right?" he said, pointing to my bag of ice.

I leered through the side of the ice bag and sighed.

Thirty Kicks in Thirty Seconds

BLACK belts warned me that it was their job to push me close to the breaking point during test preparation. It was a job that Okkie thoroughly enjoyed.

Every time I walked into the school was like playing Russian roulette. At any time, I could encounter a training day from hell.

One night I arrived to class an irritable, restless, and discontented mess. I was running late, so I gave a quick bow to the flags and trotted grumpily toward the locker room. I hated being late.

As I wrapped my perspiration-stained, red-black belt around my waist, I realized the black belt test was only three months away— and I got scared. I didn't have time to worry, though, because there was a twenty-push-up minimum for anyone tardy. When Okkie led class, the push-up penalty was thirty.

Okkie stepped up to the front of the class.

He's such a hard-ass, I muttered to myself as I whipped past classmates on my way to the mat.

We lined up, bowed to the flags, bowed to Okkie, and then sat on our knees for a short meditation. During before-class meditation, we're supposed to focus on what we want to accomplish in the next hour of training, so I tried to calm down, inhaling and exhaling long, slow breaths. It wasn't helping. My blood pumped, anxiety flashed, and an irrational rage bubbled up like a geyser. I reviewed my imperfections:

I'm lazy.

I'm moody.

I can't jump as high as Tye or spar as well as Okkie.

This uniform still makes me look fat.

The class rose from meditation and began an easy stretching routine. I could hear the boys from the earlier children's class talking loudly and excitedly in the men's locker room. They were shrieking with laughter, yelling, and horsing around as boys do—and they were grating on my nerves something fierce.

Why can't they just get dressed and leave?

While nine-year-old Julian waited for his father to pick him up, he whaled on a nearby punching bag. He thrashed the bag as hard as he could, one irritating punch at a time.

Bang! Rattle, rattle, rattle.
Bang! Rattle, rattle, rattle.
Bang! Rattle, rattle, rattle.

The noise was loud and startling, the rhythm distracting and disturbing.

For crying out loud! Somebody tell him to quit doing that!

Okkie was pleasantly oblivious to Julian's disruption. In fact, Okkie was perfectly calm as the class moved into 180-degree splits. Again, I tried to relax and focus. Over the years, I'd become extremely flexible, and a deep split was one of my strengths. But today, my negative mood kept my muscles tense and tight. I couldn't reach my usual 180 stretch, which pissed me off even more. Still, I sat wider and lower than anyone else.

"Show off," Okkie said, frowning at me. He was kidding, but I took it personally.

Okkie leaped up and led the class in a brisk run. A new green belt asked me how many laps we would run and I was about to answer her when Okkie yelled at me.

"Come on, Cathy!" Okkie said. "You're holding up the line."

Ignoring the green belt, I ran as fast as I could. It wasn't fast enough for Okkie. While my trips to Camp Mabry helped me build long-distance endurance, I still wasn't a short-distance sprinter, and I immediately fell behind him by several yards.

"Cathy! Come on!" Okkie yelled.

Now I was really angry, and without Marianna by my side, I felt like I wanted to cry or quit—or both. Part of me wanted to stop running, tell Okkie to "screw off," empty my locker, leave the school, and never return. Then I remembered Kyoshi's "Don't Quit" sign.

God, help me, I prayed.
I want my black belt.
I want my black belt.
I ran as fast as I could.
And I seethed.

I didn't run in the indomitable spirit of taekwondo. I ran in anger. I hated being pushed. More accurately, I hated being pushed by Okkie. But what really made me livid was that Okkie was right. As I looked over my shoulder, three students were running right on my heels.

I *was* holding up the line.

Our run finally ended. Without skipping a beat, we slipped right into high-speed jumping jacks, and I was relieved that Okkie was now picking on someone else. Amid the jumping jacks, I seethed more venom. I was angry—so angry I wanted to knock someone into next week. I wanted to hurt someone. I didn't understand why I was so frustrated and angry. Why did being pushed always trigger rage and make me want to quit? I felt like a defenseless child.

After a water break, the class re-formed ranks and Okkie distributed several teardrop-shaped kicking paddles. We paired up as Okkie explained a new speed drill.

He was smiling. I knew that look—that arrogant, sinister grin. This wasn't going to be pleasant.

"Thirty kicks in thirty seconds," he ordered, demonstrating a quick-step transition from one leg to the other. His legs blurred like a ceiling fan on high. "Anyone who doesn't make at least thirty has to do ten push-ups."

Okkie's answer to any physical weakness in taekwondo was push-ups.

"Ready?" he said, choosing to give commands in English rather than Korean. "Begin."

Classmates hurried through their kicks while their paddle-holding partners counted. At the end of thirty seconds, some students met their quota. Some did not and hit the floor for push-ups.

Paddle switched, and now it was my turn to kick.

"Now at your level," Okkie said to me, "you should be able to get in at least thirty-six kicks."

"Yes, sir!"

"Begin!"

I kicked as fast as I could, faster than I ever had. It was as if Okkie were holding a Bunsen burner under my butt.

"Stop!"

"Thirty-two," he said to me, shaking his head and smiling. "Only thirty-two."

I immediately fell to the mat: "One, sir! Two, sir! Three, sir! ...."

"You're gonna have to be faster than that, Cathy," Okkie said.

"Yes, sir!"

We switched the paddle several more times, and each time I got in one more kick than the last, but still shy of thirty-six.

"Push it!" Okkie said to me. "Come on, Cathy! Faster! Faster! You have to be faster!"

"One, sir! Two, sir! Three, sir!"

"Faster, Cathy! Move! Move! Pivot your foot. Pivot. Pivot!" he yelled.

"One, sir! Two, sir! Three, sir!"

Okkie shook his head. He read my comfort zone like a veteran telepathist. Okkie pushed harder, forcing me to do more, faster, with greater stamina, balance, and control. Mentally, he pushed me, pointing out what I was doing wrong—and he wasn't nice. Then he watched to see if I had the courage and desire to be better and to correct and learn from my errors. I knew he was a good teacher because I loathed him.

I wrapped my arms around my head to catch my breath. Okkie put the paddles away. The drill was over.

"O.K., look," Okkie said to me when he returned to the mat. "You're too slow. You're gonna have to work on that, aw-right? 'Cause, that's not good enough, I mean, for a black belt. You've got to be faster. Aw-right?"

"Yes, sir," I said softly.

Class was over, and I was still alive, albeit stunned, hurt, and discouraged. I felt like a pot—like a piece of clay that had been slowly slapped, pulled, shaped, and then shoved into a fire. After all these years of following an array of instructors who poked and prodded and pushed and kneaded my body and spirit like a potter on a wheel, I was still a lumpy, unbalanced, mental, physical, and spiritual mess of human clay. The big aha still eluded me. I still hung on to fear, anger, depression, anxiety, and insecurity. Although I tried to face my dragons by looking at them through the microscope of martial arts, it felt as if I were twirling out of control on that potter's wheel. How I wished the spinning would stop and someone would spread a gentle glaze of compassion, tenderness, peace, and love over me—even if I didn't deserve it.

It was heartbreaking to realize that, like an unfinished pot, I wasn't ready. I wasn't ready to wear black. I wasn't fast enough to snatch the pebble from Master Teh's hand. But unlike the times I fled from my fears, I knew I wasn't going to be at peace until I finally faced this dragon.

Kyoshi was right. I was standing amid a raging spiritual fire, and my gut told me it would hurt less if I surrendered to the fire rather than frantically fight the flames.

I am at an Olympic-sized pool with other swimmers and an instructor. The water looks cold and dark, and I know it's deep. Everyone tells the instructor the distance they plan to swim and how fast they think they can go.

"Two laps in twenty seconds."

"Three laps in thirty seconds."

I'm silent. Paralyzed. I don't know what goal to set. I'm too preoccupied with my fear of jumping into the deep water. I know I can dive to the bottom, come up, and bob, but I always slowly sink to the bottom again. Even though the instructor says she will be there to help me if I get into trouble, I can't get over the fact that the water is deep and dangerous. I know all I need to do is dive in and start swimming. I know the fear will eventually go away and I will be fine. But I'm still afraid. I lean over the side of the pool and freeze.

Walking the Gauntlet

ON a hot September afternoon, I stood in my carport with an electric saw in my hands, a long slab of whitewood pine before me, and a puddle of sweat at my feet. One by one, I methodically measured and cut nine-by-twelve-inch pieces, which I planned to break during the next day's black belt exam. (I wanted to cut twelve-by-twelve-inch boards, but Grandmaster believed that women should break smaller targets.)

Cutting wood with intention had always been good for my spirit. It cleared away cobwebs of crazy thinking.

The saw's startling whine moved in tandem with the sawdust that gently fell to the ground like winter's first snowfall. A fresh scent of pine filled the air, and as I took a deep breath, I felt awake and excited. I couldn't wait to break the boards, and I had no doubt I could. It was the two-inch-thick concrete block that I worried about. Still, I was amazed at how calm I felt amid my excitement, especially since Grandmaster moved the test date a month ahead of schedule.

As I swept the sawdust from the ground, I remembered the days of dancing on the sawdust-slathered floors of honky-tonks with Daddy. I loved dancing with him, and I loved him, too—until the drunken car rides home, the wrecks, the incarcerations, and the abandonment. After years of silence, I recently started sending him cards and letters. Thanks to lots of sober step work and therapy, my feelings weren't hurt when he didn't respond. I accepted the fact that he would probably never call or write back. He was still an alcoholic, and if I were to rekindle a relationship with him, I'd have to accept that.

I'd come a long way with Mamma, too. No longer scared of her, I now saw my mom as an imperfect but cute little portly woman who loved Chicago Cubs baseball games and could handle more bingo cards than a Hindu god. She even accepted me being gay. All along, one of her greatest fears of me being gay was that I'd die alone. She might have been miserable all those years with Daddy, but by golly, she was married. Today, she was just happy I was in a relationship. Turns out she adored Marianna.

Sweeping away the sawdust, I realized how much dust I'd cleared from my own path. I'd come a long way—through fear, anxiety, loneliness, and alcoholism. Looking back, although life was painful every step of the way, I saw now how neatly everything fell into place. If I hadn't stopped drinking, I wouldn't have met Kyoshi. If I hadn't met Kyoshi, I wouldn't have known that "can't" was one of life's four-letter words that no one should utter or believe. If I hadn't attended Kyoshi's church, I wouldn't have been forced to look at and accept myself. I'd recently reconnected with Kyoshi, and unlike Daddy, he wrote back. And if I hadn't left Kyoshi, I wouldn't have come full circle to Master Pliska and been on the verge of finally finishing what I'd started. I was even grateful to Ed. Now I knew why I couldn't get out of his grasp. Unlike the bad dude on the street, I didn't intend to hurt Ed, so my defense was never going to work.

I cut another piece of wood with attention and care. They were my boards to break, and tomorrow each one would symbolize a literal breakthrough I'd had thanks to sobriety and martial arts. One board bore a fat knot on it.

"That uniform sure makes you look fat," Mamma once said.

"You lazy American. No wan work hard," that instructor told me.

I chuckled and calmly smiled. I no longer felt fat or lazy.

As I gently stacked the fresh-cut boards against the wall of the carport, Marianna drove up in her little red truck.

"Ready?" she yelled, her truck still running.

"Yeah. Let me put the saw in the house."

For years, I'd practiced a before-test ritual. The night before every promotion exam, I ate pasta at an Italian restaurant. The meal provided valuable carbohydrates I'd need for energy the next day. After dinner, I returned home for Phase II: lighting candles, burning incense, popping an Enya CD into the stereo, and pulling out the materials needed to tidy my uniform. I ironed every inch of the fabric with love and a hint of perfection, keeping time with the smooth rhythm of Enya's soothing voice. I took deep breaths as I pressed hot steam against the pant legs and sleeves to sharpen the creases. I even ironed the tank top I'd wear underneath. I tugged on patches of the US flag and our school decal to make sure they were secure. Then I hung the complete uniform on a hanger, stepped back, and judged my work. I was satisfied with and proud of my uniform, proud of what it symbolized that I had accomplished. I couldn't wait to wear it. My classmates might not notice the crisp uniform, but I knew that if I looked good, I'd feel good. I knew that if I felt good, I'd do my best on the test.

I didn't crawl into bed until I finished Phase III: sitting before my prayer table and asking the Universe to protect my classmates and me from injury during the test. I asked that my classmates be blessed with a good performance, and I humbly offered myself to be used in whatever manner or capacity the Universe saw fit. I wanted to pass the test, but I asked for acceptance in however the day unfolded.

I awoke on test day feeling calm, warm, and protected.

This was the day I'd been waiting for since childhood, sitting on the floor watching *Kung Fu*. This was my chance to snatch the pebble from Grandmaster's hand. I was excited and nervous, yet determined.

Still having a key to the school, I let myself in an hour before test time to stretch and meditate. As I ran laps around the mat to get my blood pumping, the black belts—all of them—began filing in. I felt honored and supported.

"I wouldn't have missed this for anything," one instructor beamed. "It's about time."

"Yes, it is," I said.

I continued warming up, opting to start the test a little winded rather than nervous. Grandmaster glided into the room as royal and regal as ever, wearing a spiffy suit and tie. As he slipped off his best shoes, our eyes met, and we bowed to each other just as we had hundreds of times before. Test participants lined up as Grandmaster reviewed our paperwork. I was sweating shotgun pellets. For a second, fear crept in, and I was convinced I'd have a seizure and pass out in front of everyone. But I took deep breaths as Grandmaster gave his pretest instructions, focusing my attention on the dusty plaques hanging above his head. I wiggled my toes against the mat to feel grounded and prayed that Okkie wouldn't call the test; he always kept a quick pace.

"Okkie," Grandmaster said, motioning his hand for my nemesis to stand beside him and call the test.

Crap.

True to form, Okkie kept a supersonic pace, but my techniques were solid. My punches and blocks had the kind of power and snap that would have made Dr. Hill proud. My kicks were solid, too—until I entered the jump-kick phase. I quickly became fatigued, and my legs felt weighted and wobbly. As I tired, my spirit yells became spiritless and muffled "yups" and I worried that all those laps at Camp Mabry and the thirty-kicks-in-thirty-seconds nightmare drills weren't enough. I quickly alerted the Universe:

God, you know all those "prayer deposits" I've been making in my spiritual bank account for the past two weeks? Well, I'd like to make an immediate and full withdrawal right now, please. Thank you.

Almost immediately, a second wind emerged. My breathing steadied. Instead of huffing and puffing, I just huffed. I had enough energy for everything Okkie asked of me and even managed to show some grace. The last three techniques of the three-hundred-kick sequence were, by design, the most difficult physical maneuvers, and I nailed each of them with power, balance, and strong, room-rocking spirit yells. I knew I would survive.

Thank you, God, I whispered.

There was no time to relax. Thirty seconds later, Grandmaster called us back onto the mat for Phase III: Forms. We started with our basic form, and I performed it perfectly, kicking as high as my head. My uniform popped and snapped. The next forms went equally well, but then I lost concentration and began one form and ended doing another. Out of the corner of my eye, I saw Okkie laughing at me so hard he had to cover his face. I was able to recover enough on the next forms to regain some respect from Okkie and to satisfy Grandmaster that I knew the material.

The last form was the elegant and powerful black belt form *Koryo*. As a white belt, I loved watching Okkie crisply blaze through *Koryo*, and I dreamed of the day I'd get to learn it. Performing it for Okkie and Grandmaster was an honor, and I nailed it.

I was doing well, but no matter how perfectly I performed, Okkie would find something to tease me about. He had plenty of material after the self-defense phase. I thought it would be easy since we only had twenty techniques compared to Kyoshi's three hundred. On the first attack, I threw my classmate down on the ground with a nice thud, but my hands were so slick from perspiration that I had a hard time maintaining the wrist grab. I couldn't get a clean grip. The rest of this phase proved just as sloppy. I again tired, and all I wanted to do was sit down and breathe.

A thirty-second water break later, I was back out on that old judo mat to demonstrate our Olympic-style sparring steps. Okkie maintained a blistering pace, and I was so exhausted that I resembled a disoriented, wobbly top. I was running on nothing but heart.

I want my black belt.

I want my black belt.

Determined not to quit, I kept my yells strong and was heartened by the fact that at least I wasn't breathing as hard as my classmates.

Next, we dove right into continuous one-on-one sparring, with only a two-minute break to pull on our pads and chug some water. I felt dopey, groggy, beaten—ready for the vultures. Still, I couldn't allow myself to think about being tired. Okkie was before me in full gear, ready to take me down.

"Did I tell you I came up with a special kick just for you?" he said, with a familiar, smart-ass grin. "I'm gonna take your head off, so you better keep your guard up, aw-right?"

"Yes, sir!" I didn't have the energy to argue. I just wanted to stay as far away from his foot as possible.

Okkie was aggressive, hitting me over and over with a fast combination of kicks and punches to the solar plexus.

"Come on, Cathy!" someone yelled from the audience. "Get 'im!"

"Get in close!" another said, after which Okkie hit me hard in the diaphragm.

"Not that close!" the spectator added.

Struggling to catch my breath, I tried to evade him, but I was too exhausted, and Okkie was too fresh and fast. He dealt hit after hit, and I was defenseless, my strength waning.

"Come on, Cathy!" one instructor said.

Okkie whipped my head around with a crescent kick. I finally countered with a punch to the chest.

"There you go!" the same instructor yelled.

"*Goman!*" Grandmaster ordered, stopping the round by tapping a pencil against the examiners' table.

The following rounds were a blur of black belt after black belt kicking and punching my head and chest, yet I fought on. I dug for every ounce of energy. Sometimes I landed solid shots; sometimes I kicked in the wind. The last black belt I faced matched my build and height, so I felt assured that I'd score some points on her. At the beginning of the match, I got in some solid kicks. Thirty seconds into the two-minute round, though, I ran out of gas again.

"Stick with it," one instructor yelled. "Stay in there. Come on, Cathy!"

"Get your guard up!" my black belt opponent warned before she slapped my head with both open hands.

I was about to counter hard when Grandmaster finally yelled, "*Goman!*"

Relieved that the sparring portion was over, I wrapped my arms around my head and took all the deep breaths I could fit into my lungs. The rest of the black belts left the mat, but Grandmaster kept my classmates and me on the floor.

Sparring, in fact, was not over.

147

Now we were going to fight one another in the "A-B-C Drill." Grandmaster gave everyone a letter—I was C—and when our letter was called, we were to fight. I was so exhausted, though, that I couldn't remember anyone's letter, and continually attacked the wrong person at the wrong time.

"*Kalyeo!*" Grandmaster yelled, pausing our sparring. He looked at me, shaking his head.

"Cah-ty, you know alphabet? I don think so. You ah 'C.'"

"Yes, sir!"

"*Kyesok!*" he yelled again, ordering us to continue.

Fighting in a blurred flurry of fists and kicks, I staggered around the mat like Daddy drunkenly stumbled out of bars, feeling disoriented and powerless to stop my body from crashing to the floor.

"*Goman!*" Grandmaster finally said. "O.K. Take protectors off."

Sparring was finally over. Still, there was no time to rest. Breaking was next. A group of board holders quickly assembled around me in a circle, and I bought some recovery time carefully adjusting the height and angle of every board. I had looked forward to this part, but now I was too tired to enjoy it. I just wanted to get the whole thing over with.

Once every board was in position, I turned and bowed again to Grandmaster, telling him the techniques I planned to use to break.

"Sir, a two-board front kick, a single-board elbow strike, a single-board step hook kick, and a knife-hand strike to a concrete block."

Grandmaster nodded in acknowledgment. "Breathe control first. When you ah ready, let me know."

"Yes, sir!"

Staring at the center of the first board, I felt a tug of uncertainty toward the block. Visible out of the corner of my eye, the block was an ominous obstacle. I tried to concentrate just on what was before me.

"Ready, sir!" I said.

Grandmaster nodded to begin, and in a split second, I sliced through those boards like a knife to warm butter. I broke all boards in succession: *Pop, pop, pop.*

Droplets of perspiration fell from my chin in slow motion, splattering snowflake patterns onto the thick, light-gray concrete block below. All was quiet. I heard nothing beyond my breathing as I stared at the oblong obstacle until it became a blur of gray mass.

God, it's thick, I thought.

I was exhausted, but I believed that I was finally near the end of a long, arduous journey, so I tried to stay focused.

After years of martial arts training—complete with sore muscles and egos, jammed sparring opponents and fingers, and many moments of failure and success—my mad search for peace had culminated in this moment. A concrete block propped on top of two cinder blocks sitting on the floor of a martial arts school represented my black cauldron filled with hot coals.

"Cah-ty," Grandmaster said. "You know tofu?"

I looked up through stringy, sweaty bangs at my instructor, who sat contentedly in full lotus position at the judges' examination table. He seemed happy. My face contorted in confusion.

"When you see tofu," he continued, "den you can break."

"Yes, sir!"

I studied the block again. It didn't look anything like tofu to me. In fact, I knew it was rock-hard because I'd knocked my knuckles on it earlier that day. Still, I squatted in a deep stance, focused on the block's center as if it were marked with a bull's-eye, and readied to do my best tofu-imitation concrete break.

My now-spaghetti legs wobbled, and my hands shook like the mornings Daddy fought withdrawals. Yet I couldn't quit now. *Now* was what I had waited for all my life. *Now* was the moment—that one, fine moment—when I could finally know what Grasshopper felt like when he emerged from the temple with the sign of the Shaolin priesthood burned into his forearms.

I studied the block. Doubt set in. Panic piled on.

I think I can, I think I can, I think I can, I silently pleaded, remembering a favorite childhood story—my first example of perseverance.

Finally, I was ready.

"Ready, sir!" I announced, looking up at Grandmaster. He slowly and solemnly nodded, giving me the go-ahead to strike.

149

With a slow, deep breath, I lifted my arm, twisted my hips, and struck the block in the center with the blade of my hand as I released a loud yell.

Thunk.

The crowd, now gathered to my left and right, sighed and moaned in squeamish, unified disappointment.

"Oooh, *that* had to hurt," someone in the crowd said.

I glanced up at Grandmaster.

"Permission to try again, sir."

Grandmaster nodded his approval.

Thunk.

"Oooh," a spectator moaned.

"Ouch," another said.

I hung my head. The knife-edge of my hand throbbed. "That was hard," I mumbled.

"Cah-ty, when you break, you mus inhale den exhale three time," Grandmaster said. "Unde'stand?"

"Yes, sir!"

"Breathe control first, den try 'gain."

"Yes, sir!"

I was baffled—beginning to wonder if Kyoshi purposely left the block I broke for him out in the sun a long time or chiseled a cheat line in the center to help it break easier. The block before me seemed harder than I remembered.

I sure hope that guy at Home Depot didn't sell me a reinforced concrete block, I thought.

Concentrating on the top center of the block, I took a deep, slow breath. Sweat poured from every pore of my body, splattering drop by drop on the mat below. My chest swelled a bit when I realized that I'd created a Big Ron Hutto puddle.

"Ready, sir!"

Grandmaster gave me the nod, and I thrust my arm up, twisted my hips, and slammed my hand down as hard as ever.

Thunk.

Onlookers groaned and then whispered to each other; Grandmaster was still and quiet.

My bottom lip quivered. My nose burned. I hadn't hurt my hand, but my pride was noticeably shattered—and that block remained as solid as the Great Pyramid of Cheops.

I looked up with disheartened, watery eyes to see Grandmaster oddly nodding approvingly at me. He waved me off the block.

"O.K. Enough," he said, motioning his hand for me to get back in line.

I would not leave the temple today.

The crowd applauded and whistled as the candidates lined up, but as I stood at attention, I couldn't hold back my tears. I tried to clamp off the emotional faucet because I knew it wouldn't look good to cry during the oral portion of a black belt exam, but it was too late; the flood had started.

My perfect Grasshopper moment was nothing like when Student Caine moved the smoldering cauldron of hot coals in his final rite of passage. It was more like moving a teapot from the stovetop—using pot holders.

"O.K., Cah-ty," Grandmaster said, "tell me about improvements you made since you started training in taekwondo."

I paused, looked down at the mat, and tried to gather my composure as snot slowly dribbled onto one of my uniform's patches. I had to give my answer, even if everyone knew I was crying.

"Sir," I said slowly with a shaky voice, "I've learned that whenever I fail, not to quit—to keep trying. Perseverance. Integrity. Courtesy. Self-confidence. Self-control. Indomitable spirit, sir!"

I sobbed harder as I hung my head. There was a long silence before Grandmaster spoke.

"You know, mos' student fail on first-degree black belt test. Not only you. You ah not just the idiot."

For a moment, I stopped crying.

Did he just call me an idiot?

"First-degree black belt mean you ah ready to become official student of martial arts," he said.

I continued to cry.

"O.K. Dismiss," Grandmaster finally said.

The test was over, and with it, a flood of feelings. Classmates offered their congratulations, but I was still weepy. Then Okkie appeared. He uncharacteristically opened his arms, offering a hug. As he drew me into his arms, I cried uncontrollably, something I'd never done before Okkie or anyone at the school. Stunningly compassionate, Okkie gently led me away from the camera-snapping, videotaping crowd.

"Shhh," he said in a soft, soothing tone I'd never heard before. "Shhh. It's O.K."

Try 'Gain

I FLUNKED my black belt test.

Flattened like a pancake emotionally and physically, I crawled into bed feeling like a failure. I was ready to spend a sad, self-pity-filled sleepless night reviewing in my mind how terrible I had performed. Once my head hit the pillow, though, I fell asleep. Slept like a baby for the first time in years. And after a full night's rest, I oddly didn't awake feeling sorry for myself.

Two weeks later, the bruise on the edge of my hand had faded, the bruise in my heart was healing, and I was again before Grandmaster's examination table for a partial retest.

In his same suit and tie, Grandmaster flipped through my exam sheet.

"Show me self-defense first," he ordered.

"Yes, sir!" I shouted confidently.

My partner, Richard, stood before me—all smiles.

This time, I had a tight wrist grip and a sharp torque on every joint. I threw Richard down and around like a judo rag doll.

Bam!

Richard moaned as he landed face first on the ground.

Thud!

Richard groaned as I struck him in the solar plexus and then swept him to the ground on his back.

I flip-flopped him to the left, right, front, and back. I was in total control, and when it was over, I didn't really care about my score; I felt satisfied and happy.

"Thank you, ma'am," Richard said, bowing and rubbing his left wrist.

"Thank *you*, sir."

Grandmaster nodded approvingly, and wrote something on my exam sheet.

Breaking the block was now optional. But since I started it on my test, I couldn't walk away from it now.

"O.K. Set up for break," Grandmaster said.

"Yes, sir!" I yelled.

I turned toward the concrete block sitting in the aisle of a walk-way. I wanted to crush it badly, and I vowed that I would not leave until I literally and figuratively broke through this last obstacle.

"O.K., Cah-ty," Grandmaster said. "Breathe control first."

"Yes, sir!

I inhaled three long, slow breaths and concentrated on the center of the block.

"Ready, sir!"

"Ah you sure you ready? I don't think you ah ready. Get closer."

I scooted closer to the block.

"Ready, sir!"

"O.K., Cah-ty. When you ah ready, den you can break. Palm heel strike."

Palm heel? But I hadn't practiced a palm heel strike.

"Yes, sir!" I shouted.

In an instant, all the visualization exercises I'd done of me smashing through that block with a knife-hand strike vanished.

I took two more deep breaths, and with all my might, I twisted my hips and slammed the heel of my palm down on the top center of the block.

Thunk.

Grandmaster sighed. Instead of hanging my head, though, this time a renewed determination sprung up. I immediately asked permission to try again.

"O.K., Cah-ty," he said, pausing. "Try stomp kick."

"Stomp kick? Yes, sir!"

Grandmaster nodded once more as he uttered his trademark phrase: "Try 'gain."

I focused anew on the brick. The muffled noise of people talking in the audience faded. I heard nothing but my breath. At a sober meeting earlier in the week, I had heard, "Do not pull in doubt the seeds you sow in faith." I had to believe I could do it.

Focusing hard on that ominous gray block, I cleared my mind of negativity and breathed in all the positive energy that would fit in my lungs. A powerful force welled up inside me, at first tingling then bolting through my body. I suddenly felt awake and alive. I took a few slow, deep breaths until I could no longer contain the energy.

"Ready, sir."

"O.K. Try now," Grandmaster said.

Like I'd done so many times in class, I thrust my knee up to my chest and slammed my heel down hard with the force of a jackhammer. My foot broke through the block easily. So easily, in fact, that I was stunned.

The room erupted in applause, whistles, and cheers.

"You got it!" someone screamed.

I excitedly picked up the scattered pieces of cement as if they were Las Vegas jackpot winnings. Cameras flashed. Classmates grabbed me for hugs. I felt like a rock star.

After eight long years of training and searching, and many more years of little girl dreaming, I finally wore a black belt.

There was no crying this time.

I was elated.

I hadn't felt that happy in years.

Work, Wander, Rest

I THOUGHT that once I wrapped that black belt around my waist, the Shaolin Temple doors would magically open for me just like when Student Caine removed the black cauldron from his path in the film. I thought that all my problems would disappear and that I would be eternally happy and serene.

This was not the case.

After all the hard work, I still had not found *it*.

IN time, I turned my attention toward others. Remembering advice Hilda gave me in early sobriety ("Seek God. Clean house. Help others."), I focused on teaching youth classes for Grandmaster for a few years until he closed the school.

"Where are we going now, Miss Cathy?" my students asked.

By that time, I'd earned a second-degree black belt, yet was woefully unqualified to lead a program. Still, I couldn't abandon those kids. I took about a dozen students to train at a local YMCA.

The program grew, and eventually I opened Tao of Texas Martial Arts Institute. It was a no-frills, open-air dojo—freezing in the winter and blistering hot in the summer—and I taught hundreds of students to love every Big Ron Hutto sweat spot they left on the mat. I hung my own damn Don't Quit sign above the dojo entrance. (I even put that mantra on the back of school T-shirts.) To signal the beginning of class, I rang a small gong that hung above the threshold between the lobby and the mat. The gong didn't send out a deep, soothing vibration like the one featured in *Kung Fu*. Instead, it made a clang. But it was a gong. It was ceremonial. It was my school, and

I got to create the atmosphere I always wanted—rich with ceremonial and ritualistic rites of passage. And the first person I asked to teach a guest seminar?

Kyoshi, of course.

AS a third-degree black belt, I continued searching and praying, and my restless spirit just about drove me and my loved ones insane.

I worked hard as a school owner and instructor and knew that I was loved and respected by students and parents. The personal sacrifices, however, were steep. More and more, I spent late evenings at the dojo, and when I was home with Marianna, I was too exhausted to be a good partner. In five years, I underwent three surgeries to repair overtraining injuries, and my adrenal glands were depleted. I loathed being a business owner, and struggled spiritually over how much to charge for monthly tuition. Did the Shaolin Temple charge Student Caine fees? How do you put a price tag on potentially life-transformational classes?

Eventually, I closed the school and moved classes to another YMCA. I took periodic sabbaticals and searched for what to do next.

Answers were elusive.

I loved teaching and mentoring. I just needed to find a sane, healthy way for that love to fit into an exhausted, aging body with osteoarthritic knees and a bulging disc.

The Buddhist Temple Retreat

PROMISES are tricky things. When you make them, they become glued to every cell. Your body remembers them. They don't go away until they're kept.

Years earlier, I told my students that I'd get my fourth-degree black belt. I regretted that promise the moment I uttered the words, for that damn "Don't Quit!" sign came back to haunt me.

Every time I trained, my knees and ankles swelled, my joints stiffened, and the rest of my body ached. I felt that if I reneged, though, I'd be setting a poor example of perseverance. I wanted to age gracefully in martial arts—switch to a softer style. But first, there was unfinished business.

After many years of daily "I'm going to take the test/I'm not going to take the test" waffling, I finally found a new martial arts mentor and decided to train for the exam, damn the pain.

It had been ten years since my last rank test.

PART of the pre-test was to spend four days in silence at a local Buddhist temple.

A dormant desire to walk a spiritual path returned. Eager and excited, I couldn't wait to eat, pray, and sit in silence with the monks.

My bags packed by the door one Friday, I was ready to take a short drive to the outskirts of town to the temple. I tried to remain open-minded and not have any expectations. Earlier in the week, I'd even said a few prayers that all ended with "...and if for any reason I shouldn't go on the retreat at the temple, please intervene on my behalf."

The Universe answered.

Ninety minutes before the retreat was to begin, I listened to a voicemail from a monk going on and on about communication issues, dignitaries making a surprise visit, and the decision—with apologies—to cancel my stay.

Stunned in silence, I sat at the kitchen table with my car keys in hand. Though disappointed, I knew there was a reason for the intervention, even if I didn't know why in the moment.

But what was I supposed to do now?

Thirty minutes later, I hopped into the car and headed to a hotel on the Gulf Coast, deciding to spend as much of the weekend in silence as possible. New rules: No radio, no television, no social media, calling Marianna and responding to texts within a one-hour span in the evening, and speaking only if spoken to.

THE hotel room was quiet. Too quiet. I heard only the hum of an old air conditioner and my annoying, chronic tinnitus. Out of habit, I reached for my cell phone repeatedly, then pulled away at the last minute as if it were hot coals. It felt weird to be at the beach and not plan fun outings, and I felt sad when I realized I woke up that morning thinking I'd end my day at the temple.

Through the hotel window, I watched seagulls fly around the building. Then I noticed a cute baby gull, and was sure I never would have noticed the little sucker if I weren't watching in stillness and silence. For me, that little seagull played the role of a symbolic grasshopper at my feet.

Thank you, Universe.

Hours later, the sun long gone, I toggled between studying a book of quotations from Mother Teresa and another from the Dalai Lama. I read about the "Tree of Self-Defeat," about forgiveness, and about "freedom from mental anguish." It was as if Master Teh put these excerpts before my eyes on purpose.

Thank you, Universe.

I slept deeply and awoke rested, yet sad.

After breakfast, I strolled along a bay front seawall, where a fascinating display about planets was placed much like the Stations of the Cross. The information seemed perfectly suited.

"Craters cover the surface," the display for Mercury read. "Most are scars from the dawn of the solar system, when asteroids and comets pounded the planet. Now all is still and silent."

I've cratered before. I still have childhood scars. I've definitely felt pounded by life. And this weekend, all is still and silent. Fascinating.

"Jupiter's beauty masks turbulence. Between its colorful bands of clouds swirl hurricane-like storms."

The Great Red Spot in the display's photo was striking.

Fear has always been my Great Red Spot. I've worked hard to mask it.

Who knew I had so much in common with Mercury and Jupiter? Thank you, Universe.

At a restaurant for lunch, I wrote a letter to myself—an honest account of how I'd held myself back for years.

After lunch, I walked to the edge of the bay, tore up the pages of my letter, and tossed the paper into the water. The tiny pieces slowly sank to the bottom, some quicker than others.

I gave my worries to the water—to the earth.

How fitting that I encountered that planetary display.

The earth and its water were big enough to absorb my little worries and take them out to sea, far away. I could immediately feel some distance from the pain.

Again I slept soundly, and awoke at 5 a.m. I rose and wrote about some awakenings with old-fashioned pen and paper:

I like early morning silence.

I need to make more time for silence and meditation, daily reflection, and spiritual study.

I've enjoyed studying my books.

I meditated for twenty minutes, then dressed and took another walk to the shoreline to watch the sunrise. While waiting for the sun, I practiced the two martial arts forms I was honing at the moment: taekwondo's *Pyongwon* and ving tsun kung fu's *Siu Nim Tao*. It felt good to be out that early. I watched the sunrise, took photographs, and eventually strolled back to the hotel.

In my room, I sat on the edge of the bed, remembering my excitement about staying at the temple. Just as a black belt didn't solve all my problems, a silent retreat wasn't the answer either. But it wasn't silence I needed and craved as much as stillness. Peace. A serene spirit.

I decided to return home early.

All packed, I walked through the hotel room one last time for any forgotten items. And that's when it hit me: By the door, my packed bags were stacked the same way they were the morning I was supposed to go to the temple. My eyes stung. Warm tears flowed in a steady stream down my cheeks to my chin, then plopped on my cotton shorts. I wanted to go to the temple so bad. My heart yearned for it. I cried hard—"little girl" hard. The tears flowed from a dream so many years ago that just wasn't meant to come true. *Kung Fu* was a television series. A Hollywood fantasy. An ideal spiritual world housed in a nineteen-inch TV. I'd never find the perfect incarnation of an imaginary TV character as seen through the eyes of a tender, nine-year-old girl, and it was probably time to stop searching for something that didn't exist.

This realization hit me hard.

OLD neurological pathways die hard when implanted at such a

young, impressionable age. It took months of therapy to help me unpack all the emotions around this new reality. I needed to forgive my nine-year-old self for the years spent in agony in this crazy search for a TV fantasy. I needed to have compassion for the part of me that still wanted to believe in a mystical, magical life in martial arts.

And what about that promise? Though I still held the goal of getting a fourth-degree black belt, the non-Buddhist temple experience took the wind out of my rank promotion sails. Eventually, I busied myself with long-distance biking, hiking, and, as Hilda always recommended, service work.

Athlete Advocacy

IN the summer of 2017, USA Gymnastics wasn't the only Olympic sports organization rocked by sex abuse scandals. USA Taekwondo (USAT) was right there in the mix. One day that summer, USAT officials asked me to be an informal athlete liaison. I wanted to ensure athlete safety, so I agreed. My task? Create an environment for athletes to talk about abuse, and if they wanted to file a report, refer them to USAT, the U.S. Center for SafeSport, or local police. I wouldn't pressure anyone to file a report. I'd simply listen to their experiences and pain and educate them on their rights and options.

I banged the clichéd drum on social media to encourage martial artists to report abusive coaches and teammates, but convincing athletes to speak out proved more difficult than all my black belt exams combined. The athletes were afraid to talk. Some were still in the Olympic pipeline system and were hesitant to file formal complaints for fear of losing a potential spot on the national team. One woman was so scared and still scarred by her experience that she could only text, "I just want you to know, me too."

When one athlete finally comes forward, though, others find the courage to do the same, and the dam of silence finally broke. Athletes who had been quiet came forward on the heels of the #metoo movement. I fielded countless phone calls, emails, Facebook messages, and texts from all over the country.

Athletes (mostly women) sent statements to the U.S. Committee on Energy and Commerce and the Subcommittee on Oversight and Investigations, the bipartisan lawmakers charged with investigating abuse in organized sports. Public hearings were held. High-level executives of several Olympic national governing bodies resigned. Even the head of the U.S. Olympic Committee stepped down.

Finally, the ugliness was out in the open, and it was becoming possible to ensure the safety of current and future athletes.

Expect the Unexpected

IN Chicago the following summer, I met up with a Wisconsin taekwondo colleague and one of his students in a hotel lobby before dinner. I'd mentored his student through the reporting aftermath of an assault.

Master Steve towered before me awkwardly. His student, Alyssa, stood in the corner with her cell phone out as if to take a photograph of us.

"When I was coming up through the ranks," Steve began, "I was always told that first, second, third degree was what you've done with the sport, and fourth and beyond is what you do *for* the sport. There's nobody that I have ever met that has done more for taekwondo than you, so..."

He reached from behind and pulled out a thick black belt with four gold stripes.

"Holy crap!" I laughed in surprise.

"I present to you your fourth-degree black belt," Steve said, "because of the wonderful work you have done in advocating for our athletes and being there for them and helping make our sport better."

Steve bowed as he handed me a belt that bore the following embroidered inscription:

MASTER CATHY CHAPATY
#METOO #NOTINMYSPORT

It was a profoundly humbling moment—unexpected, yet making perfect sense. Everything had come together with and without my doing. For a moment, I felt a bit weird not having taken a physical test for the belt and of having someone other than my instructor award me such an important rank. I also winced a bit at the word "Master." (I prefer and will always remain "Miss Cathy.") Yet after I stopped hyperventilating in excitement, it all felt natural. Peaceful. I earned every stitch of that belt in ways beyond physical measure.

Now what?

IT'S been decades since the winter of 1972 when I sat on the cold hardwood floor of my family's living room—in awe of what I'd just watched on television. *Kung Fu* was deeply inspirational. It let the little girl in me believe there was a yin in the world opposite my chaotic yang home. It helped me survive childhood.

In the near half-century since, I've sobered up, gotten therapy, and spent decades dabbling in a plethora of different martial arts: aikido, Brazilian jiu-jitsu, tai chi, and two different styles of kung fu. Each art was mentally and physically challenging in its own way, and though there were pockets of serenity, none led to the perfect spiritual experience my little girl craved. Instead, a more physically fit, grown woman paid bills, pulled weeds in the yard, raised a herd of dogs with Marianna, rocked sick babies as a volunteer in a hospital's neonatal intensive care unit, and navigated a still-difficult relationship with Daddy.

All these years later, when I recall that TV pilot, I know now that it was never about holding rank. Grasshopper wore a black sash as part of a simple monk's dress. The sash bore no more significance than a western belt looped around a pair of blue jeans.

It was never about the belt.

It was about spiritual knowledge.

And for me, it was always about finding inner peace.

Today I think I understand Master Teh's words during a training scene in *Kung Fu*:

While explaining the various animal styles, Master Teh tells Student Caine, "…we remove conflict within ourselves and discover harmony of body and mind in accord with the flow of the Universe. It may take a lifetime to master...."

And so the search continues.

Of course, *Kung Fu* still offers a road map.

"What will you do?" the railroad worker asked Caine in the last scene of the film.

Caine's reply was simple. And so is mine:

"Work. Wander. Rest when I can."

Acknowledgments

THANK you to all my instructors—good and suspect—for you all taught me something of value.

Thank you to every classmate who joined me on the journey without judgment. Okkyun Sin, thank you for pushing me when I wanted to stay safely complacent. Brian Duffy, thank you for refusing me as a student and encouraging me to finish what I started. And "Ed," thanks for that early wrist-grab lesson. I love you.

I'm grateful for longtime writing peeps Sheila Watson and Kelly Stern for giving me permission to tell my story. Thanks, y'all.

Thank you to the many people who reviewed this manuscript over the years and poked, prodded, and questioned little things. Special thanks to Alicia Finn Noack, David Bordeaux, Lynne Marie Wanamaker, and Susan Strobel.

Thank you to the amazingly talented Callie Jo Prather for an awesome cover photo and design.

I'm grateful for writing mentor Donna Johnson, aka "Coach," who has always advised me to "go deeper." This memoir is better because of your support, inspiration, and wisdom.

I'm incredibly grateful for Marianna Kretschmar, the best coach and training partner in life.

Huge thanks to my sober peeps and mentors: Hilda C., Cid B., Clary K.-R., Catheran B., and everyone at the Saturday morning women's recovery meeting.

Lastly, I'm grateful for Kyoshi, who has remained in my life because of and in spite of who I am. I love you—now and forever.

About the Author

CATHY CHAPATY holds a fourth-degree black belt in taekwondo and has studied a variety of martial arts styles for more than twenty-five years. She is an Ambassador for the Association of Women Martial Arts Instructors, has led seminars for National Women's Martial Arts Federation (NWMAF) camps and is currently chair of its board of directors, and is a member of USA Taekwondo and the Writers' League of Texas.

Chapaty is the author of *No Pouting in the Dojo: Life Lessons through Martial Arts*, and has had dozens of newspaper and magazine articles published on topics ranging from anger management and integrity in sports to mentorship through martial arts. In 2012, the Embassy of the Republic of Korea honored her work for an essay on the transformational power of taekwondo.

She lives in Austin, Texas, with her wife and a herd of foster-failure pets.

Also by the Author

No Pouting in the Dojo:
Life Lessons through Martial Arts
Dudley Dog Press, 2017
(Sidekick Publications, 2014)

"The Anger Dreams Are Made of"
Pissed Off: Forgiveness on the Other Side of the Finger
by Spike Gillespie
Seal Press, 2006

Sports Planet:
Sports Played Around the World
Steck-Vaughn Publishing Co., 2003

"Mentors, Masters, and Heroes"
Power Up! Building Reading Strength
Steck-Vaughn Publishing Co., 2001

50322758R00104

Made in the USA
Columbia, SC
05 February 2019